Jesus, My Mentor

Jesus, My Mentor
A Spirituality
for Living

JOHN L. KATER JR.

CHALICE
PRESS
ST. LOUIS, MISSOURI

Bible quotations, unless otherwise noted, are from the *New Revised Standard Version Bible,* copyright 1989, Division of Christian Education of the National Council of Churches of Christ in the United States of America. Used by permission. All rights reserved.

Cover art: ©Artville
Cover design: Elizabeth Wright
Art direction: Elizabeth Wright
Interior design: Hui-Chu Wang

This book is printed on acid-free, recycled paper.

Visit Chalice Press on the World Wide Web at
www.chalicepress.com

10 9 8 7 6 5 4 3 2 1   04 05 06 07 08 09

Library of Congress Cataloging-in-Publication Data

Kater, John.
  Jesus, my mentor : a spirituality for living / John L. Kater, Jr.
    p. cm.
  ISBN-13: 978-0-827217-16-1 (pbk. : alk. paper)
  ISBN-10: 0-827217-16-1
1. Spiritual life—Christianity. I. Title.
  BV4501.3.K38 2004
  248.4—dc22

                                                        2004011567

Printed in the United States of America

Dedicated to
the students, faculty, staff, and administrators
of the Church Divinity School of the Pacific,
colleagues, friends, pilgrims

Contents

Introduction   1

1   The Spirituality of Jesus   5
     Living the Reign of God

2   Spirituality in Context   19

3   Story and Community   35

4   A Spirituality of Caring   55

5   Toward the Future   73

Questions for Individual Reflection   97
and Group Discussion

Introduction

A generation ago, the great film director Stanley Kubrick gave the world the film *2001: A Space Odyssey.* Based on science fiction by the British writer Sir Arthur Clarke, Kubrick's film fascinated its viewers with its glimpse into what life would be like at the beginning of the twenty-first century.

Kubrick's vision imagined the dawn of the twenty-first century as a heady mixture of fantasy, mystery, fear, and hope. He foresaw the beginning of a new era, comparable to the birth of civilization, where transcendent mystery and human ingenuity combined to move human history to a new level of competence and consciousness. This new era would reveal the beauty hidden in space, the music encoded in the universe, even as it raised unforeseen threats and challenges to the very place of humankind in the creation.

Those of us who admired *2001: A Space Odyssey* when it first appeared may still recall something of the wonder of trying to imagine a new century and a new millennium. Many of us were far more fascinated by the thought of exciting advances, of a new and yet unseen world, than the ominous ambiguity that was part of the film's vision. But probably none of us who sat spellbound by the dream of a new millennium could have imagined what it would actually be like. Ironically, living through the reality of 2001 revealed a world that, for all its advances, turned out to be mired as always in hard truths about us: we still wrestle with the facts of life and death.

The tragic events of September 11, 2001, and their aftermath have shaken our optimism about the new millennium. What was once the promise of a new world has been revealed as the old, battered one, but with the depths of its darkest possibilities brought home in new and often terrifying ways.

In the post-2001 world, many individuals who were once content to live life in an unreflective way, with little thought for the larger and deeper facts of life, have found themselves changed. What was once perceived as a mild hunger for a broader, deeper perspective—the gnawing interest in spirituality that has been loose in the world for a while now— has become, for many, a passion. Finding a way to explore the deep questions of life and how we live it fully has become an intense search.

In the rich diversity that is our globalized culture, there is no shortage of sources to explore in the great banquet of competing perspectives. American Christianity has multiplied denominations and sects, many of them offering a set of certainties for interpreting and responding to the history that is happening all around us. The great world religions—each with its own permutations, each with a venerable history of reflection and a set of prescriptions for living well—were once unknown to most Americans but are now readily accessible. And there is a whole spectrum of therapies, self-help techniques, diet and exercise regimens that would never call themselves "spiritual," but in fact presuppose particular ways of looking at the world and prescribe particular ways of living in it. Few of us have been untouched by the longing for a place to stand, a stable center from which to ask the hardest questions and seek a way to live more fully.

Whether or not they claim to be religious, now more than ever many Americans care a great deal about spirituality. But what they often mean by the word is a private relationship between themselves and God. It is generally perceived as a way of finding God by digging deeply into our inner depths, which is by definition a solitary enterprise. It is often grasped as a way of finding peace in troubled times, perhaps even as an escape from trouble. And it is sometimes very attractive to turn our backs on the familiar and everyday; the more unusual the approach, the better.

While such a spiritual search might be exciting, even significant, this book invites the reader to begin closer to home. Its assumption is that Christianity offers a meaningful spirituality for times like these, but many—perhaps most—people have never explored it in depth. The starting point is as near as the Bible on the shelf. This book is about the spirituality of Jesus. It is written for those who have never met Jesus or who have only vague memories of him from childhood, as well as for those who have a deeper acquaintance with Jesus, but are moved by the times to want to learn more.

This book is about how Jesus lived with God and affirms what I have come to believe: the spirituality of Jesus is not hopelessly out of date, but continues to offer a vision of life with a loving God that gives hope and meaning to us as it did to Jesus and his friends. So while it begins with seeking to understand how Jesus came to know God and how he lived in the light of God's promises, that is only the beginning. If what we believe about him is true, Jesus never kept his spirituality to himself. Excited and moved by what he had come to know about God, he *shared* that wisdom with everyone who would listen.

The spirituality of Jesus is not just an artifact of history, an interesting curiosity of forgotten religious lore. The spirituality of Jesus invites *us* on a journey full of the same kind of adventures he had. It invites us to tap into the profound wisdom that Jesus experienced.

This book begins by offering a way of coming to know the God of Jesus and of his people the Jews, the God of the Hebrew scriptures and the Christian New Testament, as Jesus knew and loved God. The God of Jesus is not the frightening or distant deity so many mistake for the God of the Bible, but the God who opens a way where there seems to be no way, who is at home in the world we call home, and who—perhaps to our surprise—does indeed welcome us back when we are lost.

This book is also not about finding God in our solitude, but in community. It is not about discovering peace by turning our backs on the world, but finding God's own peace in the midst of the world's brokenness. It is not about lost manuscripts or hidden wisdom, but about stories near at hand. It does not require the services of an especially enlightened "expert," but only attention to the message of Jesus and his friends. It is not about strange rituals or super-human disciplines, but about what we do as we meet and come to know this God together: how we share good news— which, after all, is one of the most natural behaviors in the world.

This book suggests that revisiting the God whom Jesus knew and loved might just change everything: how we treasure the world we live in, how we notice people we overlooked. It might just reinvigorate the way we work and play, worship and pray, live and die. Shall we begin?

The Spirituality of Jesus

Living the Reign of God

Now after John was arrested, Jesus came to Galilee, proclaiming the good news of God, and saying, "The time is fulfilled, and the kingdom of God has come near; repent, and believe in the good news" (Mk. 1:14–15).

Even the casual reader of the New Testament can hardly avoid noticing several significant themes that permeate its content. One is the constant reference to "good news," often translated by the old English word *gospel*. Indeed, the four books that preserve what we know about the life of Jesus are called "gospels"—"good news" as told by Matthew, Mark, Luke, and John. Far from being objective biographical sketches, they intend instead to tell a story that, it is assumed, the reader will find to be *good* news.

But while most readers of the scripture do not find that concept particularly surprising, many are nonplused when they notice what Jesus describes as "the good news," because to many modern ears, it seems strange, perhaps irrelevant. Yet unless we notice the content of the good news as Jesus understood it, we may miss his point entirely. The meaning of the verses from Mark's gospel, quoted above and which appear at the very beginning of his account of Jesus' life and ministry, is very clear: the "good news" is the announcement that "the kingdom of God has come near."

The modern spiritual pilgrim might wonder what "good news" there is in such a message. We might well ask how the language and imagery that reflects a world so distant and alien from our own could possibly give us "good news." This question deserves to be taken seriously.

In the first place, citizens of the United States, whether Christians or not, are heirs of a political and cultural tradition that honors a revolt *against* a king. If we think about kings at all, we remember the oppressive wrongs of the British monarchy as catalogued in the Declaration of Independence and against which our patriot ancestors fought and won a revolution. In our vocabulary, the language of kingship is set against freedom. A description of God in royal terms would seem more appropriate for a demanding and unforgiving deity than for a God whose presence is *good* news.

Furthermore, kings are male; in the ancient world, they were patriarchal leaders whose very word was law and whose absolute sovereignty placed them at the head of a hierarchy that dominated women, children, and slaves. Not much good news there!

Finally, we are used to thinking of a "kingdom" as a geographical place, found on a map and listed in an itinerary. Surely there is not much good news in an image that makes it sound as if God is the ruler of some obscure land with pretensions of grandeur!

What, then, are we to make of Jesus' constant use of the term "good news" that he says he came to share? I want to offer several suggestions. First, we can speak of the "reign of

God" and eliminate the overtones of patriarchal imagery and geography that cling to the notion of *kingship.* I believe that *reign* actually comes closer to what Jesus intended than does the English word *kingdom.* But even if we are willing to speak of God's "reign" rather than "kingdom," what about the idea that God is a tyrannical governor of the universe who doesn't take no for an answer? When we begin to explore the language and imagery of Jesus, he often surprises us by inverting traditional meaning in order to give an entirely *different* significance, almost as if he is playing with the meaning of the words and challenging us to understand what he means. For example, when he wanted to explain his concept of leadership, he took a basin of water and began to wash his disciples' feet—the lowliest of chores, restricted in his world to household slaves. When he entered the city of Jerusalem just before his death, he accepted the praise of the crowds and rode into the city on a donkey as if he were the king they had been waiting for; but later he stood mute before the Roman governor and died the death of a criminal. Clearly when Jesus spoke of "lordship" and "kingship," he was not using those words in the same way as his enemies, or even his friends, ordinarily used them.

The story of Jesus' experience in the desert, which follows his baptism and his dramatic coming to awareness of the mission to which God has called him, tells us that behaving as kings are expected to behave was one of the ways he was tempted to use his power for his own purposes. And the gospels make it clear that this would have been a betrayal of his calling. So we can be certain that whatever he meant when he spoke of God's reign, Jesus was specifically *rejecting* the everyday meaning of the words.

So what *did* he mean? There is an important clue in the prayer Jesus taught his followers to pray. "Pray then in this way: Our Father in heaven, hallowed be your name. Your kingdom come. Your will be done, on earth as it is in heaven." It sounds as if the phrase "Your will be done, on earth as it is in heaven" is something of an explanation of the words that precede it: *The reign of God is what the earth would be like if God's will for it were ever accomplished.* Understood in those terms, the reign of God might indeed turn out to be promising for us—if we can trust that God's will is indeed good news. Certainly Jesus believed that it was. And if God's reign is something we are to pray for rather than something God imposes on us against our will, then it does not contradict our freedom, quite the contrary. Jesus' prayer and his parables point to a God who wills good things for us, but who *invites* us rather than coerces us to seek what God promises. In other words, God's reign does not destroy our freedom; it affirms and even depends upon our freedom. The spirituality of Jesus does not point us away from the world; it invites us to hope and believe that *the world can be changed,* and that *how we live with God is reflected in how we live in the world.*

• • • • •

When Jesus spoke of God's reign, he was drawing on the hopes and dreams of generations of his own Jewish people, the spirituality formed by their experience of life with God as well as the memories of their ancestors. Jesus' own life with God was steeped in the Jewish heritage that shaped him and gave him his sense of who he was. Like all Jews, Jesus found his identity in the covenant between God and Israel that had given them their being and their history.

Long before Jesus' time the wisest religious minds of his people had come to understand that covenant as a God-given calling that carried with it a very specific mission. The people of Israel were considered God's people, not in order to enjoy special privileges, but to help make God's creative love clear to the whole world. Israel understood itself as nothing less than a "light to the nations" (Isa. 49:6).

The sign of the covenant between God and Israel was the *Torah,* the law that established how the people were to live in harmony with God, one another, and the natural world in which they lived. If the people sometimes chafed under its demands and often ignored its difficult parts, they rarely forgot its joyful aspect: every stroke, every dot of the Torah was a sign of the bond of harmony—*shalom*—that was meant to influence the life of the people.

Indeed, *shalom* was meant to be the chief characteristic of life under God's Law. We are used to translating it as "peace," but in Hebrew it conveys much more: well-being, justice, abundance, joyous harmony, the condition we enjoy when we are fully in God's presence. *Shalom* is experienced in the quiet celebration of the Sabbath rest, in the celebration that marks the victory over oppressors, in the feasts of great national holidays such as Passover, and in the moments of joy that touch families and communities.

Shalom as glimpsed in those moments is understood to be a sign of what God intends for all creation. Israel's poets, teachers, and songwriters left behind a rich deposit of hymns and visions of what it would be like to experience God's *shalom* in all its fullness. They imagined great wedding banquets, fountains of cold spring water, the whole world made new. They painted images of cities seized by a holiday spirit, and bedecked with gold and precious stones.

But those same poets and prophets were also painfully aware that the vision of God's reign had its ironic side, because it reminded them how far away from God's dreams their world was. God willed peace, but their history was often written in blood. God commanded justice, but the rich grew richer and more cruel, "buying the poor for silver and the needy for a pair of sandals" (Am. 8:6). God created in abundance, but some feasted while others starved. God promised life, but death seemed to be everywhere.

In such times, those among Jesus' people who plumbed the vision of God's reign most deeply became aware of the importance of *signs,* clues by which we can recognize and hold on to the promise and the hope of that reign. It is not how the rich and prosperous fare that signifies whether God's will is being done, but the fate of the poor, the victims, those on the margins.

The Torah marked the bond between God and Israel and spelled out concrete actions by which those most vulnerable are to be cared for. *Actions reflect values,* the values of God's reign. For this reason, the Torah commanded farmers not to sweep up the grain that had fallen in their fields at harvest time; it was to be left for the poor of the land who had no fields to harvest. The Law was especially attentive to the needs of widows and orphans because their status in ancient Israel was so tenuous. The comfortable people of Israel were forbidden to celebrate the Passover festival without being mindful of those who could not afford the lamb that was offered and then eaten; everyone was to share in the feast.

The Law of God's covenant with Israel began with Passover, the memory of the people's liberation from their slavery in Egypt and their faith that God willed freedom for them. Perhaps most remarkable of all, the Law provided for the periodic return of all property that had fallen into the hands of creditors. Twice a century, the "Year of Jubilee" commanded that lands and houses sold out of need be returned to their original owners. Their debt was at an end. There was to be no permanent gap between rich and poor, haves and have-nots. The fact that scholars doubt if this particular law was ever kept takes away nothing of its power and its intention: The God of Israel is a God of life who does not will that *anyone* should suffer want or misery. The Jews affirmed that the same God who breathed life into a world of glorious and harmonious diversity still animates that same creation with life.

• • • • •

The spirituality that shaped the religious life of Jesus and his people was a legacy formed by centuries of living with this God. Battered by history, they continued to believe that God had better plans for them. Their hopes not only were based on the occasional signs of promise of a better life they encountered from time to time but were founded even more on their memories and the story of how their ancestors had been saved, not once but over and over, from what appeared to be certain calamity. They rejoiced in the beauty of nature and identified it as God's handiwork; but they also recalled that when their ancestors had been slaves, God had brought them to freedom in a new land. No matter how terrible their situation became—and it often was terrible—they told and retold the stories of their deliverance. The spirituality of Jesus and his people was a constant looking backward in order to look forward in hope. In the retelling of the stories of how God had saved them, they could dare to look forward to the time when God would once again change their despair into promise. Remembering what God had done awakened their imagination to the possibilities of what God would yet do for them—someday. The Jewish people lived with their God in *mindful expectation* that the misery that seemed to be their lot was not God's will for them, and that the future would provide a time when God's will for them—and through them for the whole creation—would actually be fulfilled. That hope carried them as they prayed for God's reign to come, for God's will to be done on earth as in heaven.

In the context of such a spirituality, it is not surprising that good news would be nothing more or less than the discovery that what had been looked for was coming true: the reign of God so long anticipated was taking shape in their midst. Each of the four gospels insists that *Jesus is the one who brings God's promised reign to reality.*

We have already noted that Mark's gospel, the first and briefest of the four accounts of Jesus that have come down to us, begins its narrative with the good news that in Jesus "God's kingdom has come near." In other words, for Mark the very purpose of Jesus' life and death is to announce the good news that God's promised reign, prophesied and longed for, is finally at hand.

For Matthew, Jesus' identity and mission are couched most profoundly in the language and imagery associated with the expectation of the *Messiah* or *Christ*, the "anointed one" expected to fulfill the hopes and expectations of Jewish spirituality. While all four gospels identify Jesus as the expected "anointed one," Matthew's gospel most carefully interprets Jesus' life in relationship to the history of the Jewish people. Matthew begins his story by tracing Jesus' descent from Abraham and Sarah, the ancestors of Israel. Everything about Jesus happened, in Matthew's opinion, "to fulfill what had been spoken by the Lord through the prophet" (Mt. 2:15). No detail of his birth lies outside God's plan; from the call of Abraham and Sarah to the sending out of Jesus' followers to "make disciples of all nations," there is only one story by which God's purposes are taking shape in time. To ask how Matthew understood the purpose of Jesus' life and death is to ask how he conceived the purpose of Israel's own calling, for in Jesus the whole history of Israel's relationship with God was fulfilled and brought to fruition.

In the early pages of Luke's gospel, an old man who had been waiting patiently for God's "anointed one" exclaims to God that now he can die in peace, "for my eyes have seen your salvation…a light for revelation to the Gentiles and for glory to your people Israel" (Lk. 2:30, 32). Luke perceives the appearance of Jesus as the pivotal event in world history; before Jesus is even born, his mother sings with joy about his birth:

"[God] has brought down the powerful from their
    thrones,
    and lifted up the lowly;
he has filled the hungry with good things,
    and sent the rich away empty." (Lk. 1:52–53)

To enter the world of John's gospel is to leave behind the perspective of Matthew, Mark, and Luke, because John's understanding is the fruit of a different style of reflection and a distinct tradition. Yet it is remarkable that although John rarely speaks of the "reign of God," his vision of the meaning of Jesus' life and death is by no means removed from that of the other gospel writers.

In the first verses of John's gospel, a poetic meditation on the appearance of Jesus identifies him with God's life-giving intention; indeed, we are invited to think of Jesus as the *incarnation*—the "enfleshment"—of God's life-giving word that brought the universe into being in the first place. In Jesus, that divine word "became flesh and lived among us" (Jn. 1:14). The Greek word rendered in various translations as "lived" or "dwelt" carries the implications, in fact, of "pitching one's tent." John wants us to understand that in Jesus, God has "moved into the neighborhood," "taken up residence" among humankind. It is the same idea conveyed when Matthew speaks of Jesus in Isaiah's term *Emmanuel* ("God with us"). In Jesus, the closeness to God that was promised for God's reign becomes a reality.

But in his accounts of the "signs" that Jesus did among his followers, John clearly expresses his understanding of Jesus as the servant of God's reign. In each case, Jesus demonstrates access to power, beyond ordinary human possibility, that he uses in remarkable ways. The "signs" Jesus offered are to be read as demonstrations of the arrival of God's power on the human scene, signifying the fulfillment of God's purposes and Jesus' role in bringing them to pass.

If the reign of God is marked above all by *shalom*, fullness of life, it is in the signs of life-giving that John's view of Jesus is most clearly aligned with the perspective of the other gospels. When Lazarus, buried for three days, staggers forth from his grave in response to Jesus' call, John is telling us as clearly as he can: To be in the presence of Jesus is to touch the reality of God's reign. John's Jesus speaks of himself in the unforgettable image of the good shepherd who gives up his life to save the sheep. At the climax of the passage he declares, "I came that they may have life, and have it abundantly" (Jn. 10:10).

• • • • •

Surely it is not by accident that in spite of their differences in outlook, each of the four gospels recalls Jesus' spirituality as deeply rooted in his belief in, and hope for, the coming of God's reign. They do this in similar ways.

Proclaiming the good news. All four gospels affirm that Jesus proclaimed the arrival of God's reign and that this message is the good news at the heart of his life with God. Like most great spiritual leaders, Jesus was known to his followers as "Teacher." The gospels are full of parables, stories with a twist or "hook" to catch the hearer with a surprising insight about God and God's purposes for humankind. They also preserve even briefer comments, some of them only a sentence or two, in which a metaphor or turn of phrase communicates something of Jesus' vision about God's ways with us. Those ways are not a secret to be guarded, but news to be shared. What is striking about this aspect of Jesus' spirituality is the way in which he shared the promise of God's reign.

Performing signs of the reign of God. Like any great teacher, Jesus communicated his message by his words *and* his actions. God's reign was not simply an idea that he treasured; it shaped how be behaved toward others, especially those with human needs. All four gospels describe how Jesus performed "signs" to indicate the nearness of God's reign. In doing so, they understood him to be presenting his "credentials": "But if it is by the finger of God that I cast out the demons," he tells a hostile crowd in Luke's gospel, "then the kingdom of God has come to you" (Lk. 11:20). That is surely how his contemporaries would have understood stories such as the feeding of the five thousand (Jn. 6:1–14) and the wedding at Cana (Jn. 2:1–11). To them the jars of fine wine and the feasting on loaves and fish were not magic tricks, but signs of the abundance that they believed was God's will for them.

Celebrating God's reign. The lavish abundance of the reign of God seems to have been a welcome theme in Jesus' life. His actions, like his words, move easily to celebration. In Luke's gospel, when he reflects on the divine joy at the return of those who had distanced themselves from God's promises, he tells not one but three related stories of loss and return: a shepherd returns to the fold with a lost sheep (Lk. 15:1–7); a woman seeks and at last finds a lost coin (Lk. 15:8–10); a son alienates himself from his father and is welcomed back with feasting (Lk. 15:11–32). In each case Jesus the teacher sees the joy, and the celebration it occasions, as an image of God's ways with us.

Clearly Jesus' followers remembered him as one for whom the gospel of God's reign was truly *good* news, joyful news. Even at the solemn moment of his death, its outcome is foreshadowed in the celebration of joy and freedom represented by Passover. However bleak his own circumstances, however bitter the reality of the Jewish people under Roman occupation, Jesus marked that night by feasting and singing hymns of celebration. We cannot narrate the story of Jesus' betrayal and crucifixion without reference to the Passover memory of liberation and the celebration of life in the face of the threat of death.

Identifying the signs of God's reign. The lavish outpouring of blessings that Jesus associated with the reign of God kept Jesus from being mean or restrictive about its implications. Others (including some of his closest followers) may have worried about who could, and who could not, share in the feasting God promised. The gospels remember Jesus as one who invites the most unlikely of guests to join in the celebration, and who rejoices when God's purposes are made real, no matter at whose hand. If his disciples had difficulty getting beyond a possessive attitude toward the reign of God, and even speculated about their own favored position within it, Jesus noted how God's blessings fall on those who deserve them and those who do not. God's reign is served, he pointed out, not by pious words or even by correctly identifying Jesus, but by those whose actions help make God's reign become a reality. Jesus was more concerned about identifying signs of the reign of God than about restricting them to his own words and deeds.

Pre-figuring the reign of God. Just as Jesus' life was dedicated to serving God's reign, he called into being the community that was also directly related to that mission. Jesus belonged to a people convinced they had been called to serve God's purposes. The little group that accompanied him on his travels, and the much larger community that soon were called "Christians," shared this belief that they were meant to live on behalf of the promise of God. Jesus' followers understood that their community was *to be a sign of the reign of God* and of the values of that reign. If his friends were invited to serve one another rather than competing for privilege, it was because their life together would serve as a sign of how God intends for the whole creation to live in harmony.

Denouncing the enemies of God's reign. Jesus identified with the service of God's reign and his understanding that *shalom* means fullness of life, which drew him inevitably to those whose own claim to life was tenuous and for whom, therefore, the promise of God's reign was most certainly *good* news. All four gospels depict him as at home with those who were outcasts, victims of the prejudice and scorn of the powerful and comfortable. We need only consider the cast of characters in his stories and the story of his own life. Over and over, he gives life to someone who has been touched and scarred by the power of death. Illness, rejection, terror, and scorn are death's faces; they are signs of its power as surely as Jesus' acts are signs of life.

But it is impossible to take seriously the *promise* and the *gift* of life at the heart of Jesus' spirituality without also being aware of the *threat* to life signified by the faces of death. If he announced the reign of God, he also *denounced* those who opposed it, especially those who used their privilege or power to abuse others in God's name. The gospels portray Jesus as one who speaks judgment against those who oppress, mistreat, and degrade other human beings.

This is most clear when he attacked the merchants and bankers who profited from the pious Jews' coming to purchase animals for sacrifice or to change their money for temple currency. "It is written, 'My house shall be a house of prayer'; but you have made it a den of robbers" (Lk. 19:45).

Resisting the power of death. Jesus' life was a struggle on behalf of life and against death; there were times when that struggle took the form of resistance. We might see Jesus' brave celebration of the Passover as an act of resistance on behalf of life in the face of death. In Jesus' time the heavy hand of the Roman Empire controlled the Jewish people, occupied their land, ridiculed their religion, mocked their culture, and reduced them to poverty through taxation. Jesus lived his entire earthly life in a land dominated by the ominous presence of Roman soldiers, a corrupt Jewish puppet-king who served Rome's interests, and a colonial bureaucracy that took the best of what his people produced. Yet when Passover came, Jesus and his friends did not despair at Rome's apparently unbreakable power; they remembered the night when their ancestors crossed the Red Sea and danced before the God who had saved them. Every observance of Passover under occupation was an act of resistance and a celebration of courageous hope.

Jesus' last Passover night ended with the appearance of the soldiers sent to arrest him, the screams of torture, and the death of God's "anointed one." His willingness to pay this ultimate price of faithfulness to God's reign over against the pretensions of any earthly power is an act on behalf of the reign of God and the victory of life over death. Resistance, as people in many settings since Jesus' own time have affirmed, can be a powerful gesture on behalf of life. When no word can be spoken, silence is its own message. It was a lesson that Jesus' followers were called on to remember in many times and circumstances.

• • • • •

This summary merely touches on the significance of God's reign for Jesus' spirituality as described in the four gospels. But if all four gospels do, in fact, interpret Jesus' life with God as a calling intimately related to the coming of that reign, it will not surprise us to discover that same vision shaping the way his followers interpreted their own world and attempted to serve God and others while living in it.

Those who heeded Jesus' call to come and follow found his resurrection from the dead to be the greatest sign of all that God's reign had begun. In its light, they experienced astonishing situations and unforeseen circumstances. But they accepted whatever happened to them as part of the ongoing story of their life with God and the coming of God's reign. And what is more, for those individuals who follow Christ and understand the story of their own life with God in relation to the story of Jesus, God's reign has already begun. They share in that victory over death; the promise is already on its way to becoming true. "So if anyone is in Christ," wrote Paul, "there is a new creation: everything old has passed away; see, everything has become new" (2 Cor. 5:17).

2

Spirituality in Context

The stories of the Jesus we meet in the four gospels help us understand how Jesus lived his earthly life with God and in the service of God's reign. Those stories culminate in Jesus' resurrection. His disciples and friends soon realized that after the resurrection, their life with him would not go on as before. Everything changed. On one hand, the New Testament writers shared a profound conviction that Jesus was still alive, though in a new and barely comprehensible way. Most, perhaps all, expected him to return soon, to right the wrongs of the past and to complete the mission of establishing God's reign on the earth. At the same time, they knew that their own lives continued to be lived out on the same stage as before, but without the daily face-to-face presence of the one in whom they had placed their trust and to whom they often deferred.

What we know about the unique period that followed the resurrection can be inferred from the letters Paul wrote some twenty to thirty years after those events. The events receive their most detailed treatment, however, from Luke, who wrote a companion volume to the gospel that bears his name, in which he told the story of how faith in the risen Christ moved into the wider world of the Roman Empire.

Reading Luke's second volume, known to us as The Acts of the Apostles or the book of Acts, does more than carry on the narrative of the aftermath of Jesus' life, death, and resurrection. It also demonstrates how Luke understood the life of Jesus' followers as *preserving the spirituality* that had shaped Jesus' life: a way of looking at God and the world in the light of God's promise of a new heaven and a new earth. Like his contemporaries, Luke found clues to help him understand what Jesus was about by rereading the Hebrew prophets, especially the latter chapters of Isaiah.

Writing at one of the bleakest times in all Israel's history, the author of those chapters lived with the survivors of brutal defeat and the destruction of Jerusalem and its temple. Exiled to their conquerors' capital, they found themselves living through conditions similar to those their ancestors had known during the worst times of slavery in Egypt. Devastated by their defeat and the apparent hopelessness of their condition, they sang bitter songs like the one preserved in the book of Psalms:

By the rivers of Babylon—
there we sat down and there we wept
    when we remembered Zion…
O daughter Babylon, you devastator!
    Happy shall they be who pay you back
    what you have done to us!
Happy shall they be who take your little ones
    and dash them against the rock! (Ps. 137:1, 8–9)

But it was Isaiah's genius to rise above the despair and to rediscover hope as he recalled what God had done for Israel in the past. As those memories lifted his spirits, he dreamed of a new time when God's will would once again be done as in the days of the exodus.

For I am about to create new heavens
>   and a new earth;
the former things shall not be remembered
>   or come to mind...
I am about to create Jerusalem as a joy,
>   and its people as a delight.
I will rejoice in Jerusalem,
>   and delight in my people;
no more shall the sound of weeping be heard in it,
>   or the cry of distress.
No more shall there be in it
>   an infant that lives but a few days,
>   or an old person who does not live out a
>   lifetime;
for one who dies at a hundred years will be
>   considered a youth,
and one who falls short of a hundred will be
>   considered accursed.
They shall build houses and inhabit them;
>   they shall plant vineyards and eat their fruit.
They shall not build and another inhabit;
>   they shall not plant and another eat;
for like the days of a tree shall the days of my people
>   be,
>   and my chosen shall long enjoy the work of their
>   hands.
They shall not labor in vain,
>   or bear children for calamity;
for they shall be offspring blessed by the LORD—
>   and their descendants as well.
Before they call I will answer,
>   while they are yet speaking I will hear.

> The wolf and the lamb shall feed together,
>> the lion shall eat straw like the ox;
>> but the serpent—its food shall be dust!
> They shall not hurt or destroy
>> on all my holy mountain, says the LORD.
>>> (Isa. 65:17–25)

Luke, Paul, and the other followers of Jesus made sense of their understanding of who Jesus was in the light of promises such as these. As they recalled what Jesus had said and done, they interpreted those memories as the beginning of that *new creation* for which their ancestors had longed. And perhaps even more remarkably, they saw themselves caught up in that promise.

In the early chapters of the book of Acts, Luke describes how the first disciples found themselves transformed from hesitant, frightened followers into energetic, courageous *leaders* and *advocates*. The story of Pentecost recounts how they became aware of God's power, the power that had made Jesus an advocate of God's reign, present among them. Surely we are correct in seeing the images of fire and wind in Acts 2 as giving to the disciples what Jesus had received in his own baptism: a strong sense of being chosen by God and of receiving what was needed to accomplish that mission. That assumption is affirmed when, shortly afterward, we see Peter and John speaking powerfully about the promise of God's reign and healing a paralytic beggar (Acts 3 and 4). Though Jesus is no longer physically present, the promise of living in the light of God's reign goes on. And the signs that make the promise tangible continue.

To those who came after Jesus, the ways in which Jesus lived his life with God in the light of God's reign became signs that confirmed the promise of which Jesus had spoken. Jesus' way of understanding what it is like to live with God spread from a small group of believers and became a powerful force throughout the Roman Empire and beyond. That movement could never have happened without memories and hope, promises and signs.

Reading the history of that movement with care, we might find two things that engage our attention. One is the way in which the spirituality of Jesus continued to shape the life of his followers far beyond the time and place in which Jesus lived. The other is the way by which that spirituality took root in those strange new settings and gradually became "at home" in ways that Jesus' friends might never have foreseen.

Within a few years, for example, Jesus' followers were wrestling with the relationship between the ancient faith of their Jewish ancestors and the eagerness of the Gentiles to know and share the promises of Jesus.

Luke gives form to this struggle at several points in the book of Acts, especially in the story of Peter and his encounter with a Roman centurion (Acts 10). At first glance, no one would seem to be a less likely subject for learning to see the world and God as Jesus taught than an imperial military officer. After all, he represented the cruel military occupation under which Jesus had been executed and which continued to impoverish the Jewish people. Most Romans had nothing but scorn for Jews and their religion. Christians, like other Jews, feared and hated the people who had brought misery to their people. Furthermore, like all Gentiles, Romans were considered "unclean"—their very touch made it impossible for the Jews to approach God without undergoing a ritual of purification.

But in a troubling dream, Peter receives an astonishing insight: the old distinction between "clean" and "unclean," which had been at the very heart of Jewish identity and sense of mission, does not fit into the vision of the radically welcoming God whose loving care extends to all creation. In the unsettled frame of mind brought on by this dream, Peter does something he probably would never have dared to do otherwise: he welcomes the Roman soldier and his companions and actually begins to tell them about Jesus. To everyone's surprise, the Romans receive the Holy Spirit—that is, they begin to manifest the signs of God's presence and power which the disciples had encountered at Pentecost.

Surely we can understand the episode between Peter and the Romans as a sign of God's reign, recognizable because it is similar to other signs we see in the gospels. Yet it is different as well—indeed, radically different because it involves telling the good news to those previously outside the people among whom Jesus moved. It is true that the gospels give us glimpses of Jesus' healing Gentiles, even Romans; but he did not invite them into his circle or say that they would become followers of his way of seeing and living. Already, ten chapters and only a few years into the story of Jesus' followers, something has changed dramatically. The good news has been told in a new and unknown context.

The later history of the Christian movement demonstrates vividly that sharing the spirituality of Jesus and its expectation of God's reign in different contexts is not always easy. There is usually a tension between wanting to hold on to Jesus' perspective and the recognition that some elements of that perspective were specific to his own time, place, and culture. Many Jewish Christians were appalled by Peter's behavior in extending hospitality to Gentiles. Yet it would seem that the first of Jesus' followers found themselves in the (perhaps uncomfortable) position of trying to explain God's promises to those who had never heard them and who lacked the basic knowledge and history on which they were based.

That challenge is made both easier and more difficult when we remember that we do not experience the fullness of God's reign, but rather its signs and clues. That means that our awareness of God is always partial and tentative. We do not have access to the fullness of God's being; otherwise we would be God, not human! Perhaps that is why Jesus carefully recognized and identified those signs, even when they were not necessarily evident to his companions.

The spirituality of Jesus is a way of thinking about God and God's ways with the world. This spirituality assumes that those signs are very important for helping us move deeper into the mystery of God. The signs Jesus offered, as well as those he pointed out, have several traits in common. First, they are always *temporary* glimpses of God's purposes for the creation. When a small boy offered five fish and two loaves of bread and five thousand people ate until they couldn't eat any more, we are correct in taking that gesture as a powerful sign of the abundance that is associated with God's reign: the assurance that the world's hunger is not God's will. But the next day, everyone who shared that banquet was hungry again. Jesus did not short-circuit natural laws or jump over history to the end of all things; he created a moment when people could glimpse and experience God's will for humankind. Even the most dramatic signs, such as the various stories in which Jesus raises the dead, are *temporary*; we must assume that Lazarus and the widow's son and Jairus' daughter eventually grew old and died like everyone else. The reign of God remains as an unfulfilled promise, beckoning us toward the future.

Second, the signs identified with Jesus always happen at moments of extreme tension between the way things are and the way they would be if God's purpose were fulfilled. At the wedding in Cana of Galilee, the sign offered when vats of water suddenly ran with the finest wine occurred at a moment of tension between the joy and celebration of life represented by a marriage and the shame and scarcity associated with a family whose supply of wine was running low. The many healings recorded in the New Testament speak to the tension between the will of God for fullness of life and the pain and sufferings which are often the lot of human beings. We might even say that we are most likely to experience signs of God's reign precisely at those moments—and in those contexts—when the present reality cries out loudest in contrast to the purposes of God summed up in the concept of *shalom*.

Third, Jesus' words and actions are always dramatically contextual. For twenty centuries, Christians have been arguing over whether the advice or directions Jesus gave to individuals in the gospel stories are universal rules for everyone. When a wealthy young man asked Jesus what he must do to live fully in God's reign, Jesus told him to sell everything he had, give it to the poor, and follow Jesus. Some hearers of the story down through the ages have argued that Jesus meant what he said, not only to one rich man but also to anyone with financial resources. But in fact, what Jesus did and said seems to have been very specific in its application. Certainly we can discern a point of view, a set of values and priorities, drawn from what Jesus believed about God and God's reign; but his application of them depended entirely on the circumstances. After all, Jesus did not heal every sick person who crossed his path, or feed everyone who was hungry, or ask that all his followers lead itinerant lives. It is surely impossible to fathom why Jesus did what he did at any given moment; but a profound attention to specifics points toward taking with absolute seriousness the context in which individuals live and work and which shapes their struggles to live faithfully

We know that Jesus' human understanding of God, shaped by his own experience and the traditions and hopes of his people, gave him a passion to tell what he knew about God and to invite others to cling to the same promises for which he lived (and died). His vision of a God who is forgiving, welcoming and infinitely attractive gave him a particular insight into how God must notice and draw near to those whose lives are most distant from the promise of God's reign: the poor, the ill, the suffering, the lonely, the despised. His own habit of seeking out people whom others scorned, and the harsh words he used toward those who mistreated them, demonstrates what a profound consciousness of justice informed his sense of *shalom*. For Jesus, the peace of God was not a quiet, meditative solitude, but rather the harmony of people far off being brought near. And it was not an abstract kind of justice, but a sense of the profound dignity and value of every human life that crossed his path and the compassion such a sense evoked.

We might say that Jesus' spirituality is rooted in a particular understanding of creation, and of humankind's place within the creation. In spite of his respect for the heritage and vocation of Israel, he seems to have been able to identify and respond to human need whenever he encountered it. Most dramatically, his encounter with a Gentile woman who insisted that he heal her daughter gives us a glimpse of Jesus' own growing awareness of the wideness of God's mercy and care. Much later, when Christian theologians began to reflect in a more ordered way on the implications of insights such as these, they were struck with the ancient Hebrew perception that, in spite of human differences, "God has made of one blood"[1] all the nations of the earth. More specifically, the many cultures which form the global mosaic in which we human beings live together not only divide us; they also share a great many elements in common, and all are related to God in principle. That is to say, every culture has value, and in many ways affirms the compassion, the justice, the celebration of life which form the destiny of humankind. Yet each culture also has elements that drive a wedge in the oneness of the creation, that glorify violence and hate, that glorify some at the expense of others. This "doctrine of creation" depends upon our awareness of Jesus' own spirituality, his sense that Israel's vocation was not for itself alone, and that God's love casts an ever wider net. The books of the New Testament beyond the gospels give us fascinating glimpses into how his first followers became increasingly aware of what it means to speak of the God whose very name is love.

---

[1]*Book of Common Prayer* (New York: Seabury Press, 1979), 100.

Future generations of Christians also made much of the fact that Jesus lived out the values of God's reign, not in some abstract ethereal realm but (as the Apostles' Creed puts it) "under Pontius Pilate," that is, at a very specific moment in human history and the history of his people. It is useless to try to speak of Jesus' spirituality apart from his own tradition and culture. The God with whom he lived and in whom he trusted is the God of Israel, who set a people free, brought them home from exile, and continued to sustain them under brutal Roman occupation. That is why it makes no sense to consider the spirituality of Jesus without paying attention to the faith of his people and the scriptures that nurtured it.

But if Jesus' spirituality is shaped by and rooted in his own culture, then it must be possible for that point of view and way of life to take root in any culture; otherwise, the reign of God would depend on being a first-century Jew. It used to be fashionable for Christian thinkers to point out how appropriate the world in which Jesus was born turned out to be for the propagation of his beliefs. For all its cruelty, the Roman Empire provided secure transportation, effective communication, a "peace" based on its lordship over many peoples who had previously been at war with one another, a widespread network of language and culture that made it possible for people in the mountains of Syria and peasants in the north of France to speak to one another. But the specificity of the Jewish setting in which Jesus was born is much more important, the assurance that God comes to be with people in their time of need, when history would seem to be their enemy.

That is something of what Christian theologians mean when they speak of *incarnation:* that in the person of Jesus, the very *human* figure of Jesus, God's own values and dreams and passion for life *take flesh* in a very specific, concrete human life. But just what does that mean for *our* spirituality?

First, it means that living with God does not require that we reject or ignore the circumstances of our life, but rather, that those circumstances become the raw material of our life with God. The very concrete poetry with which Jesus' ancestors and friends spoke of God's reign should help us to see how the everyday world becomes the raw material of our life with God. Perhaps no story Jesus told makes the point better than the one about the good Samaritan (Lk. 10:25–37).

In that story, the piety of the priest and Levite required that they ignore the (possibly dead) man lying in the gutter, because contact with a cadaver would make them ritually impure. It is the Samaritan who demonstrates what God is like, providing a powerful illustration that God's image is not restricted only to *some* human faces and that life-giving spirituality takes human need with absolute seriousness. God—the reality of God, the promise of God, the compassion of God—makes sense to people in the absolute concreteness of their own life and context. It is for this reason that we must identify the spirituality of Jesus as a *contextual* spirituality.

Second, the spirituality of Jesus is a *shared* spirituality. The vision of God's reign that shaped the nature of his relationship with God is itself a shared vision. It is impossible to find anywhere in the pages of the Hebrew or Christian scripture the slightest hint that our destiny with God is a private affair. Perhaps this is one of the hardest of all learnings for Christians in North America, steeped as we are in the radical individualism of our own context.

The very nature of Jesus' calling to serve God's reign made it imperative that he draw a community around him to share his vision. Indeed, as we have seen, that community itself was meant to be a sign of the *shalom* of God. Jesus' first followers used a variety of images to stress that the kind of life with God they had learned demanded a community.

Perhaps the most potent of them all is Paul's image of the body of Christ. Christ is the head, and all those who have drawn near to follow him—to share his vision of who God is and what the world might be—are the many parts that make it possible for the body to function.

As with all such images, the full meaning of "the body of Christ" has many dimensions. To describe a community as Christ's body means that there is, on some level, a fundamental unity between Christ's very identity—his life—and that of the community of his followers. Of course, such an image cannot help but highlight the profound differences between the singleminded faithfulness of Jesus and the failures, selfishness, and conflict that have always haunted those who came after him. Nevertheless, it seemed to Paul and his readers that the passion and purpose for which Jesus lived and died were to continue to be the motivation of the community that formed around him, even though he was no longer physically present to urge them on. Just as the gospels record that Jesus sent his disciples out to do what he had done and thus to serve as his representatives, so Paul considered himself and the others who followed Jesus to be sent out with the same mission: to share the good news of what God has in mind for the whole creation.

Identifying Jesus' followers with the members of the body enabled Paul to exert a powerful brake on the human impulse to consider ourselves more important, even crucial, to the functioning of the body. No one is called to serve God's reign as Jesus was called; rather, each has been given very specific gifts to *participate in* creating and identifying signs of the new creation among us, to celebrate the possibilities we find for knowing it more fully, and to resisting whatever violates that reign. Plumbing the metaphor to its depths, Paul reminded his readers that no body can function effectively unless it has all the requisite parts; just as it needs eyes, ears, heart, liver, so the community entrusted with serving God's reign needs a variety of members and the gifts they have been given.

Eyes do not *choose* to be eyes, Paul might have said, ears do not *choose* to be ears. No more do we, who have also been gifted with special traits and abilities that can be useful in serving God's reign, *choose* the role we have been given. The spirituality that lies behind the image of the body of Christ is a perspective and a way of life that notices, recognizes, and affirms the gifts each of us has been given, and searches for ways to use them in serving the purposes of God's reign.

But here too the *context* for living in the light of God's reign assumes great importance. The gifts we are given are to be used on behalf of God's reign precisely in the setting we call home. We are not called to follow Jesus in the first-century Palestine in which he lived. Those of us who are caught by Jesus' invitation to follow his way of seeing and living are called to do so where we are, not in some place that is either more exotic, or more comfortable, than the place and time where we live.

Another image that made much sense to the first Christians was that of the *church*, not in the sense we often take it as the building or institution dedicated to God's purposes, but in the primary meaning of the word. Behind the image of "church" in the New Testament is the Greek word *ekklesia*, which means "those who are called." It reflects a central experience of the early followers of Jesus. Most, perhaps all, were aware that while they had made a commitment to God's reign, however tentative, the initiative did not come from them. Rather, it seemed to them that they were *responding to God's invitation.*

That sense of being *called* is most obvious in the stories of the Twelve, the special companions of Jesus who were with him from the beginning. All four gospels agree that those who stayed close to him did so because he invited them into that position. Paul first appears on the scene as one of the primary enemies and persecutors of the church, driven by his understanding of the demands of his own faith to hunt out followers of Jesus and turn them over to the appropriate authorities. The fact that he lived the last years of his life as a tireless advocate of God's reign as it was made clear in Jesus does not represent a deliberate decision to change his mind; it reflects his sense of being *called,* much to his surprise, to serve the reign of God as Jesus had taught and embodied it.

That same sense of calling pervades the pages of the New Testament. Its men, women, and children found themselves within the number of those who saw themselves as having passed, as Paul said, "from death to life" because they accepted Jesus' vision of God and the world as their own. They reported that they had heard God's invitation, God's call, and they responded in fear and joy. In doing so, they also found themselves caught up in adventure, danger, and celebration.

• • • • •

Christians continue to find meaning, comfort, and encouragement in their efforts to serve God's purposes by sharing the life of the community we have come to call the church. When the church is intent on serving God's reign, people find there a setting for identifying the gifts God has given them, and ways to put them to use on behalf of God's vision of the new creation. But first they must hear the good news that God does indeed have plans for this world, news that frequently comes through stories that awaken hope. Those stories may be drawn directly from the pages of the New Testament; but they also may be drawn from the efforts of faithful people to use their gifts.

Stories and hope: Whatever the context in which we live, we can experience the dynamic between stories and hope, between hope and taking an active part in remaking the world. Paying attention to context means learning to hear stories in ways that help us see the world around us with new eyes, and to conceive of possibilities where the human imagination might fail. The pattern is clear: Stories lead to *hope,* which in turn leads to *action.*

The story of the Christians in any given context can become part of the collection of stories we might call the lore of faith. Their story is profoundly *theirs,* it belongs deeply to them; but in telling and re-telling it, it becomes part of the *shared memory* of the Christian community, the body of Christ.

It becomes a story that can awaken hope in others who live very different settings, and in the process might well move them to share the good news of God's reign in their own context.

This is the way of God's good news: When we hear and tell the stories that make God's purposes clear, hope is born. And when hope is at hand, the signs of God's reign come into being before our eyes.

3

Story and Community

The good news of God's reign lit up the world of the New Testament and changed both the people who heard it and their way of seeing God, the world around them, and themselves. To read their story is to encounter the dramatic nature of that change. They discovered a new sense of who they were, and how God could use them in bringing a new world into being. Frightened fishermen became steadfast leaders; corrupt officials set out to rectify the wrongs they had committed; greedy and selfish men and women became generous and compassionate.

But the stories of the New Testament happened a long time ago, in a world that seems very different from ours. The question we must ask is, Can the good news that once changed them also change *us*? If the signs of God's reign that fill the pages of the scriptures were by their very nature contextual and temporary, what can they possibly have to do with us? How can that story become our story?

35

One thing is certain: If the stories of our ancestors in faith are to have any reality for us, we will have to do more than read them. Otherwise they are only literature, of the same category as the classics we encountered in school or college. What is called for is a setting that will do more than pass on the stories; we need a setting that will somehow open them up, make it possible for us to enter deeply into them, to make them our own, and in the end to become part of the story.

We are familiar with the image of the author closeted in an attic, crouched over a typewriter or a computer in silent isolation, only to emerge months or years later clutching a sheaf of papers now ready to be shared with the world. That is not how the stories in the New Testament came into being. All four gospels were written in the context of a particular community; the context shaped their point of view and the way the stories were told. The profound interest in the Jewish tradition we find in Matthew's gospel tells us that he wrote it from a perspective rooted in a community made up of people who understood and respected that tradition. We now know a great deal about the various churches that served as settings for telling and retelling the stories that conveyed the good news of God's reign. The more we learn about them, the more obvious it is that the stories in the gospels were meant to be *shared*.

In the same way, both the book of Acts and the letters from Paul and others bear witness to the importance of a *community* for passing on the good news. Paul's letters cover a wide variety of issues and questions precisely because they are addressed to churches with different customs, characteristics, and personalities. It is remarkable how similar they can seem to congregations we ourselves may have known. Some are more religious than others and preoccupied with "getting things right." Others wonder how to live as Christians in a cosmopolitan and sophisticated world with very different values. Others are excitable, or seem to be mired in controversy and conflict; still others are struggling to get along in settings with the rich and poor, powerful and powerless. At times we can catch something of Paul's frustration as he struggles to answer complicated questions, or to bring peace to those who seem to be determined to be at one another's throats.

But in spite of the inevitable frustrations that are part of community life, at no time did Paul—or anyone else we meet in the New Testament—ever suggest that living the spirituality of Jesus was a solitary endeavor. To the contrary, they worked hard and long to hold fragmented communities together, to keep people within "the household of faith." Paul and his colleagues understood that being part of the community—the body of Christ—is not a by-product of Christian faith, nor is it an "optional extra." Being part of the body is what we do because we have *heard the good news,* and so that *we can continue to hear the good news.*

That good news has always been communicated to people in the form of *stories*—the story of God's people and their life with God; the story of Jesus, his life and death and his rising again, and the stories of his friends. In fact, the Bible is the story of life with God in the light of the promise of God's reign. Even those parts that might seem to be anything but story—laws, census figures, hymns, sermons, letters, proverbs—are, in fact, an integral part of the one story. It is the story of how the good news of God's reign is heard, told and retold, revised, argued with, and told yet again.

When we read the story of Jesus' friends in the aftermath of his resurrection, when they no longer had the certainty of his immediate physical presence, we find them struggling to remember and to pass on the stories. What we call the "sermons" that appear from time to time in Acts are in fact more storytelling than preaching; we hear Peter and Paul and Stephen and Philip retelling the stories of Israel and Jesus, and struggling to explain their meaning. For the people who responded to them and were drawn into the community of Jesus' followers, those stories communicated the good news. The stories showed the signs of God's reign happening to others just like them. The stories were no longer just *ideas*, but pointed instead to *a way of life*.

Through the stories of God's reign, the friends and followers of Jesus began to understand that God's good news mattered for them. In effect, they became part of God's story. When we read their stories in the New Testament, we are reading "scripture." But when those men and women were living through their own experiences, they were living the stories; they were acting in ways that made sense and became signs of hope to those who came after them. Paul didn't know he was writing "epistles"; he thought he was writing to his friends. But the real-life adventures and dramas and conflicts that he labored over have become part of the story of the community—the body of Christ.

Memories that Jesus' followers held from the early days of the community were tales of persecution, but also of public affirmation of the story they had come to believe was true. There was hardship, but also sharing, mutual care, and a remarkable willingness to entrust themselves to the community. Many years later, writing in *Acts*, Luke described those early days in these words:

> All who believed were together and had all things in common; they would sell their possessions and goods and distribute the proceeds to all, as any had need. Day by day, as they spent much time together in the temple, they broke bread at home and ate their food with glad and generous hearts, praising God and having the goodwill of all the people. And day by day the Lord added to their number those who were being saved. (Acts 2:44–47)

A few chapters later, Luke returned to the theme of the common life of Jesus' followers.

> Now the whole group of those who believed were of one heart and soul, and no one claimed private

ownership of any possessions, but everything they owned was held in common. With great power the apostles gave their testimony to the resurrection of the Lord Jesus, and great grace was upon them all. There was not a needy person among them, for as many as owned lands or houses sold them and brought the proceeds of what was sold. They laid it at the apostles' feet, and it was distributed to each as any had need.

(Acts 4:32–35)

We know, of course, that even that intimate group of Jesus' friends and followers was not without conflicts. But even so, we twenty-first century Christians might be struck by several elements of Luke's reminiscences of what he must have seen as "the good old days."

One noteworthy aspect of the story *is the immediate relationship between the story of Jesus and the life of his followers.* What held the group together was the "testimony" of those who had known him, who had been present with Jesus and who had firsthand memories of the resurrection. It was their telling and retelling of the story of Jesus that drew people more and more closely into the community associated with him.

Second, *being touched by the story of Jesus drew people into a community.* There is no reason to think the men and women who responded to the story were any more religious, virtuous, or "holy" than anyone else. To the contrary, we know from the hints about them scattered through the pages of the New Testament that they were ordinary people, with jobs and families and hopes and secrets and regrets, just like anyone else. And yet, Luke looked back to a time when people were so moved by the story of Jesus that they made radical changes in their lives, uprooting their families, leaving their jobs, even selling their homes and possessions and sharing the proceeds with other followers. Being touched by the story of Jesus changed their priorities, their values, their behavior.

Responding to Jesus and his story involved dramatic changes in their life; it involved a conscious and freely-chosen lifestyle, a way of living shaped by the memory of who Jesus was and how he himself had lived. It is for this reason that his friends were first known as followers of "the Way": the way of life that is the way of Jesus, the way of life lit up by hope and trust in the promises of God's reign. And it is why, very soon, people began calling them "Christians": the people who identify themselves with reference to Jesus the Christ. And while they were clear that they had chosen to follow the new Way, at the same time they may have felt that the choice had not been theirs but God's.

Even many years later, long after the early intimacy of the first Christian community, Jesus' followers still relied on one another in hard times, sought out one another when they were alone in an unknown city, and gathered regularly to share meals and to recall the story of Jesus.

Third, if the story of Jesus and his life with God was at the heart of their community, if the promise of God's reign remained alive in their expectations, *the community itself became a sign of the promise of God's reign.* The gathering of Jesus' followers, fragile yet determined, was not only called into being by God for a purpose; it was the very body of Christ, an instrument of the continuing presence of God's love in the world.

This must have been both an astonishing claim and a profound challenge to the little group of Christians who held on to their hope and told the stories that gave them life. It is one thing to pass on someone's values or way of life, especially if the person is someone we respect and even revere. It is something else entirely to try to live out those values ourselves! Yet the image of the body of Christ makes it clear that for Jesus' followers, life with God is not simply something that Jesus followed, but is for anyone who accepts Jesus to follow. So the kinds of behavior that so preoccupied the early Christians—how to be generous, how to be forgiving, how to be agents of healing, how to invite others into their community—were not merely pious exercises. They were ways of telling the good news. The life of the church becomes an integral part of the story. In the end, we cannot separate the story of Jesus from the story of his followers. The spirituality of Jesus, as he lived and taught and died to make God's reign real, becomes the spirituality of his followers. Their life is shaped by seeking and finding the *shalom* they identified with God's reign. And as they live out that spirituality, they not only retell the old story; *they become part of the story.* They tell the story in the living of their lives. Their own adventures with God become part of the longer, deeper story of how God's reign comes to take shape, not only in the Israel of Jesus' time, but in every time and place.

Congregations: Signs of the Reign of God

Reading the stories of our faith ancestors in the New Testament can be an exercise in both amazement and doubt. It is hard not to be impressed with the generosity of those who shared not some, but all their resources with the fledgling church. The tireless journeys of Paul and the other apostles, the catalog of hardships and persecutions they endured, the sacrifices they willingly accepted, border on the heroic. But those more public efforts rested upon the dependable support of many others, most of whom we know only by name if at all. Paul could not have survived without the shelter and protection of other courageous but anonymous Christians.

We also know that the first decades of the early church were not all "glory days." Perhaps the memory of a single-minded and compassionate community as Luke described it in the first chapters of Acts has been improved over time; after all, Luke was describing events of half a century before, and all of us tend to have "selective" memories. Certainly Paul's letters to the first churches are full of strife and conflict, strong egos and stubborn wills, self-indulgence, and even spiritual arrogance that can still shock us today. Can anyone really claim that such a contentious community could be "the body of Christ"?

We would not be honest if we did not ask ourselves, *Just how relevant are those memories of twenty-plus centuries ago to a time and place like ours?* Just look at the issues that concerned them! Can Christians eat meat that has been offered to idols? Must all Christians follow the Jewish Law? Does following Jesus require circumcision, kosher food, and all the rest? Figuring out a way to distribute food fairly to Greek- and Aramaic-speaking widows may have been a crisis for Christians in Jerusalem, but it is hardly a hot topic for us today.

As we trace the rapid growth of the Christian movement through the first century of its development, we realize that times and circumstances have changed from the days when Jesus and a band of friends walked the roads of Palestine. The immediacy of their expectation—that God's reign would surely be established in all its fullness even as they watched— faded as they realized that the promises of that reign were not to be fulfilled overnight, but rather that they were being invited to identify with those promises—and to help them be fulfilled.

Just as Peter and Paul astonished everyone, as they spoke in the temple after Jesus was gone from the scene, by carrying on Jesus' message and his work, a new generation of leaders emerged to continue to invite people around the Roman Empire to change their lives and to take seriously God's promises of a new world. Those people—the leaders and the ones who responded to them—populate the story that carries on the spirituality of Jesus into a new generation.

Wherever the story was shared and accepted, the men and women who were drawn into it gathered together in communities, to become "the church in Corinth," "the church in Rome," "the church in Ephesus." These are the groups to whom Paul and the other writers of the first century wrote, reminding them about their new identity. "So we, who are many, are one body in Christ," Paul wrote to the Christians in Rome, "and individually we are members one of another" (Rom. 12:5). "For in Christ Jesus you are all children of God through faith," he wrote to the church in Galatia. "There is no longer Jew or Greek, there is no longer slave or free, there is no longer male and female; for all of you are one in Christ Jesus" (Gal. 3:26, 28). A passage in 1 Peter speaks of the Christian community as

> a chosen race, a royal priesthood, a holy nation, God's own people, in order that you may proclaim the mighty acts of [Jesus] who called you out of darkness into [God's] marvelous light.

> Once you were not a people,
>   but now you are God's people;
> once you had not received mercy,
>   but now you have received mercy. (1 Pet. 2:9–10)

These verses capture some of the astonishment many felt at having been invited to share the life of Jesus' followers. Any temptation to pride or a sense of superiority is canceled by the reminder that while this invitation carries privilege, it is the privilege of being offered the call to share the good news of God's reign with others: "to proclaim the mighty acts of [the one] who called you out of darkness into... marvelous light."

What are we to make of these eloquent, almost grandiose, descriptions of the church from the same individuals who criticize its members for their venal behavior, their selfishness, their lukewarm commitment, even their cluelessness?

It would seem that the leaders of the early Christian communities, marked by human failings and limitations themselves, carried a clear vision of the purpose of the communities of Jesus' followers, their call to carry on the story and to embody it in their life together. Yet they also understood the realities of those communities, knowing that they were composed of ordinary men and women, touched by

God and the vision of God's reign, but not always living up to that calling. They recognized that how a particular community witnessed to God's reign depended on the circumstances of its life. But they were convinced that sharing the spirituality of Jesus meant sharing the promise of God's reign. It meant living with and for *shalom*.

Some of the first churches struggled mightily to make that *shalom* a reality. The insistence on noticing the plight of those who suffered under the economic or social restrictions of the Roman Empire frequently raised questions and created controversy. Behaving as if everyone—including slaves, widows, children, former prostitutes, all the categories of disdain that marked Mediterranean society—was a child of God and an heir of the promises of God's reign brought many tense moments, and even persecution. The New Testament reads like an extended adventure story, as the implications of the spirituality of Jesus are taken seriously by more and more individuals, who are drawn into the story until it becomes their own.

How were they to embody the values of God's reign in their own community? Paul and others considered that the first imperative of *shalom* was *unity*. There are times when Paul seems impatient with the controversies—the *disunity*—that marked so many of the churches he knew well. If only everyone would agree to see things his way, the problems would be over! But at his best Paul knew very well that the unity of a given church was not about always agreeing, but on *how* they disagreed. Forming parties or pressure groups identified with strong personalities was not the way to remain together; in his letters, Paul argues over and over for an attitude of respect between those who disagree, the respect that demonstrates an awareness that no matter how different their opinions, they recognize one another as children of God and members together of Christ's body. Paul himself had bitter disagreements with the other apostles, notably a sharp confrontation with Peter; but neither of them ever considered for a moment that the other had placed himself outside the body of Jesus' followers. They assumed that the faith in the promises that had changed their lives forever held them together, no matter how violent their disagreements, no matter how strained their relationship, no matter how heated their words. Such a profound commitment to the community could only mean that *membership in the body is itself an integral part of claiming the promise of God's reign,* a way of living the story by which the promise of that reign comes into being.

What can twenty-first century Christians claim of the passion and commitment our ancestors in faith knew as they gathered together in community? There is no doubt that the spirituality of Jesus as it was passed on to his friends and followers is a spirituality rooted in community. If we have grown up in a culture that enshrines individualism, we may find it challenging to learn to think of the community, rather than ourselves, as our primary point of reference.

Making the spirituality of Jesus our own is in part coming to appreciate the importance of the Christian community in forming and nurturing our faith. It is learning to value the community that keeps on telling the stories that help us to hope. Most of all, claiming Jesus' spirituality for ourselves means letting ourselves be drawn into the story that community is telling and allowing ourselves to become part of it. This means learning to see the world through eyes trained in recognizing God's reign in times and places where it is not immediately evident. It means permitting our lives to be drawn, ever more deeply, into the good news until we ourselves become signs and agents of God's reign. But how can this happen?

There was a time when Christians had no problem identifying with a community of faith. Living in small and isolated villages, they gravitated toward the local church, where they gathered regularly for worship and marked all the significant events of their lives: birth, baptism, marriage, death. In times of war or epidemic or natural calamity or celebration, the ringing of the church's bell called people to gather for prayer. There was no clear boundary between the community of faith and the group with whom people lived their whole lives.

Some people still live in that kind of close-knit community. But most of us do not. For most Christians in North America, family and friends are dispersed across a continent or even in other countries. The people who live near us may have very little in common with us beyond geographical proximity. They may speak a different language or come from a different part of the world. Even if they share our language and our background, they may have a religious allegiance that is quite different from ours, or they may have none at all. There is no one place, no one community, that binds us all together in times of great joy or suffering. Most of us do not worship in the place where our grandparents were baptized and married and buried; we may not even know where to look for that place, if it ever existed.

In that sense, perhaps we have more in common with those first Christian followers of Jesus than with the believers who lived during the centuries when Christian faith was a homegrown, village phenomenon. The Christians of the New Testament found their way to the community where the story was told in ways that made sense of their life, that gave them hope and meaning and purpose for their life. In the same way, we twenty-first century Christians must find the community that makes the story of Jesus and his followers come alive for us, and invites us to make it our own. For most of us, that community will be a *congregation.*

Congregations are local gatherings of Christians who are often related to larger groups known as *denominations.* In one way or another, they share a common understanding of the Christian story. For the most part, denominations institutionalize some of the differences of opinion that have divided the Christian movement over the centuries, as well as other divisions such as ethnicity, nationality, or culture. We might say that denominational differences are a monument to the failure of Jesus' followers over the years to exercise that *shalom* for which Jesus and his friends prayed. In our own time, Christians are gradually coming to realize that what holds them together is more important than what divides them. The differences have to do more with what we emphasize than with any ultimate failure to agree on the significance of the promises of God's reign.

But the existence of so many different denominational traditions does mean that twenty-first century Christians have multiple options for community. Sometimes Christians are so frustrated by the inability of the community to maintain its unity that they choose to form their own independent churches. This gesture often has the advantage of making the sense of immediate unity more profound, but it also often makes communication with Christians in other places more difficult because the independent congregations remain isolated.

So those who desire the spirituality of Jesus have two challenges. One is to understand the importance of a community of faith in claiming that spirituality. The other is to find the community that makes the promise of God's reign come alive in ways that speak to us, drawing us into its story that is so much broader and deeper than our own small stories. For most of us, that community will be a congregation that it is part of a much wider Church that stretches around the world, back to the time of Jesus, and forward into an unknown but promising future.

At the heart of our membership in the Christian community are two *sacraments:* baptism and the Eucharist. They are signs in the here and now of God's reign among us.

Baptism: Membership in God's Reign

Followers of Jesus easily recall the story of Jesus' baptism by John as the moment when his mission in the service of God's reign was made clear, and he received God's powerful

Spirit to enable him to fulfill that mission. From the earliest days of Christian community, baptism became the sign of entrance and membership for those who were drawn into the story of Jesus and identified with it. Indeed, Paul spoke of baptism as the way by which individuals are "made one" with Jesus, so that his story becomes ours. "So if anyone is in Christ, there is a new creation: everything old has passed away; see, everything has become new" (2 Cor. 5:17).

The immediate connection between baptism and identifying with Jesus and his story is spelled out best in Paul's letter to the Christians in Rome.

> Do you not know that all of us who have been baptized into Christ Jesus were baptized into his death? Therefore we have been buried with him by baptism into death, so that, just as Christ was raised from the dead by the glory of the Father, so we too might walk in newness of life. For if we have been united with him in a death like his, we will certainly be united with him in a resurrection like his. (Rom. 6:3–5)

For the first Christians, being baptized—identifying with the story of Jesus—meant receiving a new identity, a new spirit, a new citizenship.

> But you are not in the flesh; you are in the Spirit, since the Spirit of God dwells in you…If the Spirit of [the One] who raised Jesus from the dead dwells in you, [the One] who raised Christ from the dead will give life to your mortal bodies through [the] Spirit that dwells in you. (Rom. 8:9a, 11)

> For all who are led by the Spirit of God are children of God. For you did not receive a spirit of slavery to fall back into fear, but you have received a spirit of adoption. When we cry, "Abba! Father!" it is that very Spirit bearing witness with our spirit that we are

children of God and if children, then heirs, heirs of God and joint heirs with Christ. (Rom. 8:14–17a)

Paul considered that those who have sealed their identification with Jesus through baptism have been drawn into the community filled with God's own Spirit, the source of the energy and vision that draws them into the service of God's reign. *They are already living as if God's reign were here and now.* Jesus' story has become their story, and their ultimate allegiance is no longer to any family or state or institution but to God's own reign. In an empire that took the privileges of citizenship very seriously indeed, early Christians knew that "here we have no lasting city, but we are looking for the city that is to come" (Heb. 13:14).

Bread, Wine, and Community

For all the clashes of opinion and personality, the congregations that have carried on the spirituality of Jesus understand that their reason for being is to embody and create signs that proclaim God's intentions for the world. They are confident that they have received God's Spirit precisely in order to carry on Jesus' mission. Nowhere are their hopes more emphatically remembered than when the community gathers to remember Jesus in the shared meal of bread and wine. Paul asked the Corinthian Christians, and all Christians:

> The cup of blessing that we bless, is it not a sharing in the blood of Christ? The bread that we break, is it not a sharing in the body of Christ? Because there is one bread, we who are many are one body, for we all partake of the one bread. (1 Cor. 10:16–17)

For the earliest followers of Jesus, steeped in the memories of Israel, the bread and wine they shared to remember Jesus seemed like an echo of Passover, the festival of liberation that also included bread and wine in remembrance and celebration. When they gathered for their meals, they certainly

:alled the last Passover supper Jesus shared with his friends, the meal at which he identified the broken bread and the poured-out wine with his own body and blood, his life given for the sake of God's reign. The disciples probably did not immediately understand that gesture in the whirlwind of emotions—fear, excitement, guilt, anxious hope—of their last night with Jesus. But they obviously held on to the memory; it became the heart of the gatherings of Jesus' followers almost immediately. Though its meaning has been questioned and disputed, the memory still remains.

Many of the arguments about remembering Jesus in a meal of bread and wine have focused on how we are to perceive the elements of the meal. Just *what did Jesus mean* when he took bread and said, "This is my body"? What did he mean when he blessed a cup of wine and added, "This is my blood"? And what did his friends mean, what did Paul mean, what did the Christians who came later mean when they repeated the gesture and the words?

Like all symbols, this sharing of bread and wine defies a full explanation. If words were enough, Jesus would not have needed the symbol. Yet there are some obvious hints that help us make the symbol our own. They have less to do with what happens, or does not happen, to the bread and wine, and a great deal more to do with what happens to those who share in it.

Body and *blood*, of course, are no different than saying "flesh and bones." Jesus' body and blood are simply *who he is:* the human being in whom God's promises begin to come true, the instrument of God's reign who becomes it principal sign. Sharing the body and the blood of Christ implies taking on— taking in—his very being and identity in a profound way. Surely Jesus' offering his friends that bread and that wine was a means of helping them identify themselves with him, and identify with his mission, since his death was the price he paid on behalf of God's reign.

But just as Passover was a night of terror and death, yet also the moment of liberation, so the death of Jesus is caught up in his resurrection and the new creation it begins—the sign of God's reign that changes everything. Sharing bread and wine in memory of Jesus becomes not only a sign of his commitment to God's reign, but—since Christ has been raised from death—a sign in celebration of that reign.

When the first Christians gathered in fear to remember Jesus and to retell his story in the breaking of bread and the sharing of a cup, they were deepening their membership with one another in the community of God's reign; they were, as Paul said, "discerning the body"—they were making themselves aware once again of what it means to share the life, the story, and the mission of Jesus. It was this gesture of memory and hope that energized them and made them willing signs and agents of God's reign. It was both the sign of, and the means toward, its *shalom.*

The societies in which Jesus and his companions lived were rigidly organized by categories of status, by ethnic and religious differences, by carefully calibrated hierarchies which determined the relative value of individual human beings. In the Roman Empire, Romans mattered more than anyone else. Throughout the Mediterranean world, men were more valuable than women or children; free people were worth more than slaves. Jews considered themselves more honorable and respectable than Samaritans. The wealthy looked down on the poor.

We certainly cannot claim a kind of modern-day equality for the churches of the first century, as if contemporary democratic impulses had somehow appeared twenty centuries early. Custom dies hard, and there are still many remnants of status-consciousness in the writings that preserve the memories of those communities. Yet the life of the Christian community challenged and often ignored those distinctions. The *shalom* they embraced made leaders of the poor, recalled Jesus' compassion for children, elevated women to positions of authority and respect, saw Samaritans as agents of God's own love and care, and called slaves "brother" and "sister." In spite of their failures, those followers of Jesus understood that God's reign made *all* people heirs of its promises. God, James observed, has "chosen the poor in the world to be rich in faith and to be heirs of the kingdom that he has promised to those who love him" (Jas. 2:5).

It would be hard to imagine a more dramatic sign of the profound bonds among Jesus' followers than the gesture of sharing bread and wine. In the stratified world of the first century where status was all, declining to share a meal was a way of keeping distances intact. People who shared a meal were friends or family—*companions* ("those with whom we share our bread"). The followers of Jesus broke bread and drank wine together because they belonged to one body, and because they were striving to embody what they believed God meant for all of us.

There is another link between the sacramental meal and the promise of God's reign. The gesture of a shared meal also serves as a reminder of the intimate connection between the reign of God and the promise of abundance to a hungry world. "Give us today our daily bread," Jesus taught his friends to pray. Just as the early church's concern to feed anyone in need was a concrete sign of that promise, so is the sharing of bread and wine—what later Christians came to call the *Eucharist*—a sacramental sign of that reign. Sharing the signs of Jesus' life is a reminder that there are hungry people still waiting for the promised feast of God's reign.

In the aftermath of Jesus' death and resurrection, communities of people who hoped for God's reign found in their life together a reminder of the story of Jesus. Indeed, they found that they themselves were living that story, making it their own.

Brought into a close relationship with the story of Jesus and those who shared it through baptism, they continued to act it out as they broke bread and drank wine with others who were drawn from the cosmopolitan Roman world and its rich diversity. Inspired by the story and energized by the communion they experienced with one another, they set out to be signs of God's promises. They dared to be agents of God's *shalom*.

It happened to them. It can happen to us.

A Spirituality of Caring

Claiming the spirituality of Jesus for ourselves means identifying with the story of Jesus and the good news it conveys. It also means allowing ourselves to be drawn into a community that is shaped by and represents that good news.

Thanks to the New Testament, we know well how the communities of Jesus' first followers told the news of God's reign with their lives. In their search for *shalom*, a unity that drew together people of different backgrounds and social standing, in their concern to respect those who were often scorned, in their care of the poor and needy who crossed their path, in their steadfast resistance to the inhuman institutions that claimed sovereignty over them, they became signs of what they hoped for.

But the twenty-first century world is vastly different. How can Christians today live in communities that communicate God's reign in our times?

A Priestly People

The author of the first letter of Peter described the church he knew as "a chosen race, a royal priesthood, a holy nation, God's own people" (1 Pet. 2:9). Contemporary Christians are used to thinking of priests as clergy, a specific group *within* the body of the church as a whole. Some might be confused by the author's description of the *community* as "a royal priesthood." The author was not writing about clergy, but referring to a people who function together as priests. What is at the core of this is the most basic meaning of priesthood: choosing to stand at the point of contact between God and the world as "go-betweens," communicating to others what we have come to know and believe about God, bringing the needs and concerns of others to God. This was exactly the place Jesus occupied: In his teaching, in the signs he acted out, in his courageously facing death, he was telling what he had come to know about the God of love who desires a new world. In his life with God, he brought the pain, the fear, the wants and needs of the broken lives he met into contact with God's own love and mercy and *shalom*. To be an agent of *shalom* is a priestly role; to speak and act in the service of God's reign is to claim the priestly calling of Jesus.

This understanding of priesthood goes far beyond the experience of Jesus or even of the church; indeed, whenever people communicate God's love to others, they are acting out what one New Testament scholar has called "the universal priesthood."[1] For Christians, that universal priesthood is made dramatically vivid in the life and death of Jesus and in the community that continues to be the body of Christ.

Every congregation is made up of people who have identified with Jesus' story through baptism and continue to

---

[1]L. William Countryman, *Living on the Border of the Holy: Recovering the Priesthood of All* (Harrisburg, Pa.: Morehouse, 1999).

be strengthened in their commitment to that story through the shared meal of bread and wine. Every congregation is called to be a sign of God's reign; to embody God's *shalom* in their life; and to create, identify, and celebrate the signs of God's reign all around them.

Just *how* a congregation committed to the spirituality of Jesus will live out that calling depends entirely on its context. The ability to serve God's reign depends on several important factors.

The first is a deep *understanding* of the context in which the members of the community live and work. We have noted how Jesus' own ministry, and the ministry of his first followers, was always contextual. Jesus rarely made generalized pronouncements directed toward people in general; nor were his own actions on behalf of God's reign made "in general." The words and the behavior of his friends were equally specific. They were always addressed to real individuals, concrete situations. One of the reasons the New Testament is at once lively and difficult to understand is that the ways in which God's reign was acted out were so immediately attached to a given time and place.

In the same way, serving God's reign in our time depends entirely on where the community of faith is located. Certainly congregations can learn from one another; discovering similar challenges can provide both encouragement and a source of practical advice. But in the end, no two congregations will serve the reign of God in precisely the same way—any more than the life of the church in Rome twenty centuries ago looked just like that of the Christians in Corinth or Jerusalem.

Because Christians are always bound—whether or not they remember it—to a global human family and the web of life that enlivens our planet, congregations may find themselves involved in serving God's reign in distant places. But the immediate demands are those of which we have firsthand knowledge, the context we call home. Sometimes Jesus' followers suppose that the most important ways of serving the reign of God are those activities that happen immediately within the confines of the church. Individuals who take on responsibilities for the church's administration or worship may come to consider those duties as their primary work on behalf of God's reign. But in fact the signs that most occupied the attention of Jesus and his followers were not those that happened within their own group. Even something as important as the Eucharist is not an end in itself, but a means of celebrating and embodying God's reign so that we recognize possibilities for service beyond the boundaries of the congregation.

Peter, John, Paul, and the other followers of Jesus acted out their service on behalf of God's reign in very different settings: the marketplace, the street corner, in homes and workplaces, on ships and in prisons, all over the world as they knew it. They understood that God's reign is served not merely by signs that are sheltered from the gaze of outsiders, but by public words and actions. Most Christians will find their primary opportunities for serving God's reign where they live, work, and play; as they raise their children, carry out their jobs, interact with their neighbors, read the newspaper, exercise their political duties, make choices about how they spend and save and give away their resources.

Gifts and the Reign of God

Another important factor in how congregations serve God's reign is the nature of the spiritual gifts that are present among the members of the community. Awareness of the particular gifts shared by the body of Christ was one of the foundations for what Paul taught about the nature of the church. He considered that the presence of God's Spirit among the church's members assures that the gifts necessary for the work will be present.

Now there are varieties of gifts, but the same Spirit; and there are varieties of services, but the same Lord;

and there are varieties of activities, but it is the same God who activates all of them in everyone. To each is given the manifestation of the Spirit for the common good. To one is given through the Spirit the utterance of wisdom, and to another the utterance of knowledge according to the same Spirit, to another faith by the same Spirit, to another gifts of healing by the one Spirit, to another the working of miracles, to another prophecy, to another the discernment of spirits, to another various kinds of tongues, to another the interpretation of tongues. All these are activated by one and the same Spirit, who allots to each one individually just as the Spirit chooses. (1 Cor. 12:4–11)

Paul was clear that, whatever the particular challenges faced by the dynamic—and divided—community in Corinth, God had assured that the members had the gifts they needed to accomplish their mission and to serve God's reign as their situation demanded.

We can see from Paul's letter to his friends in Corinth what gifts he considered crucial for their ministry. It is interesting but not surprising that when writing to communities in other places, Paul's list of urgently needed gifts is slightly different. For example, in Ephesus the special gifts and ministries called for were "apostles, some prophets, some evangelists, some pastors and teachers" (Eph. 4:11). For the Christians in Rome, the list includes "prophecy, in proportion to faith; ministry, in ministering; the teacher, in teaching; the exhorter, in exhortation; the giver, in generosity; the leader, in diligence; the compassionate, in cheerfulness" (Rom. 12:6–8). In each case, these were the special gifts needed to strengthen the whole community, in order, as the letter to the Ephesians commented, "to equip the saints [i.e., the church's members] for the work of ministry, for building up the body of Christ, until all of us come to the unity of the faith and of the knowledge of the Son of God, to maturity, to the measure of the full stature of Christ" (Eph. 4:12–13). The words are clear: God has graced the congregation with those gifts needed to make sure that the whole community is equipped to undertake the service of God's reign.

No doubt the list of gifts needed by any contemporary congregation in order to fulfill its own ministry on behalf of the reign of God would be somewhat different from those found in the New Testament. But the purpose of the gifts is the same: building up the community, so that all its members can be engaged actively in serving God's *shalom*.

The life of any congregation, then, has its own rhythm. This is the rhythm of *gathering* and *scattering*: gathering to break bread and drink wine together, to hear once again the story of Jesus, and consider what God is calling them to do and to be; scattering to live out that story and to serve the vision in a multitude of settings as varied as the circumstances of the members themselves.

The Gathering Community

A congregation of contemporary Christians works to develop a strong sense of how God's reign needs to be served in its context—what signs of that reign are most needed in order to communicate the good news. Then it also works to define the most important gifts needed to inspire and move the community to respond to those needs.

Reading clearly and accurately the congregation and the context in which it is called to serve God's reign is one of the basic elements of any congregation's faithful life together. Who comprises the congregation? What is its size, and is the congregation geographically concentrated or diffuse? What differences are present among its members? Economic or class differences? Racial or ethnic differences? Long-time members and recent arrivals? How do they relate to one another? How does the congregation fit into its location and culture?

In examining the broader context of ministry, the location and culture of which it is a part, a congregation needs to have a clear sense of the history of that place and of those groups that comprise it. It might be useful to ask what important historical factors continue to be significant for the distinct segments that comprise any community. (Here we are talking about community as a geographical and cultural entity, not the Christian community specifically. How, for example, would historical memories be different for farm families whose ancestors experienced the Dust Bowl; African Americans in a large metropolitan area or a small town; Haitian, Guatemalan, or Salvadoran refugees; Mexicans in Texas; Cubans in Miami; Russian or Ukrainian immigrants; Native Americans living on a reservation?)

Awareness of a context for ministry means understanding the special values, institutions, traits, habits, and customs that shape it. How do people live—on farms or ranches, in private homes, in apartments? Is the community growing, declining, or static in population? What are the celebrations that punctuate the seasons, and how are they observed? What roles do the school system, sports, a military base, a particular industry or business play in its life? Who are its heroes, its most respected figures, the role models for young persons, the individuals who appear on the front page of the newspaper or in the local news? How do people get their information? What newspapers are most read? What kinds of music do people listen to? What movies do they see? What are the preferred styles of entertainment? Do people hunt and fish, go camping, attend concerts or races, play baseball or tennis or golf, visit the beach or the ski slope? What are the other churches and religious institutions like? And are there common elements in the answers to these questions, or is the community so diverse that the answers are complex and full of unknowns?

Finally, and only when the answers to these questions have been absorbed, can congregations ask themselves how God's reign might be served in such a specific context.

One aspect of that mission is identifying and celebrating the signs of the reign of God that are already present. What examples of healing, of abundance, of mutual concern mark the community? It is part of the congregation's calling to notice where these are in evidence, to name them, and to celebrate them.

But surely there will be other aspects of any community's life that can be identified as "pressure points" when seen in the light of the values of God's reign. Who are the people who are overlooked, forgotten, or despised? To use the rich symbolism of the scriptures, who are the "victims of death"? Who suffers discrimination or injustice? Who lacks access to the plentiful abundance that God intends for all people? Where are the earth's beauty and its resources being violated, abused, hoarded? Who are the ones who are suffering—whose body or mind or spirit is broken?

And finally, as a congregation plumbs the depths of its community, it must ask *why*. Why are some people victims of death in all its forms? What are the complicated facets of the community's life—its institutions, its inherited prejudices, its gap between privilege and want, its unspoken entitlements and denials—that create suffering and want? What are the roadblocks to change, and how can they be discovered and named? These questions might seem far removed from the story of Jesus; yet if we read the New Testament with care, we will discover that Jesus and his first followers were very conscious of the complex dynamics of evil that turned some of God's children into victims. They could not adequately create signs of God's reign, or resist what stands against it, unless they understood these dynamics. Neither can we.

The perspective of our Christian ancestors was not limited to the immediate circumstances they saw before them. Behind all the scenes of compassion and conflict that fill the stories of the New Testament were the global realities that shaped individual lives: the constant awareness of the power of the Roman Empire, the economic and social upheaval its policies caused, the ambiguous stance of the religious authorities, the powerful individuals and parties and groups whose long shadows hovered over everyone. How can we understand the death of Jesus without being aware of those larger forces? How can we fathom the generosity of Peter in accepting an invitation from a Roman soldier unless we take account of what the Roman Empire would have symbolized to him? How can we appreciate the cost of faithfulness unless we have a sense of the treasure of a Roman citizenship and the meaning of subordinating it to God's reign as Paul did? In the same way, as we explore the facts of life in our own community's context, we must be aware of those larger forces, both positive and dangerous, that are working to mold and shape it.

One of the primary reasons for the congregation to gather is to hone awareness of the wider community of which it is part, to teach one another to notice both strengths and weaknesses. This means observing those elements of life that must surely cheer the heart of God, and those aspects that cry out for the promise of God's reign; examining both in the light of the story of Jesus; and pondering together what that story invites them to do in the light of these promises. Certainly the increasing clarity about the positive and negative dimensions of its context will move a congregation to prayer; but members will also want to ask how to set about identifying and creating signs of God's reign that will change the texture of life for themselves and their neighbors. A congregation whose spirituality begins from the vantage point of God's reign will resist whatever contradicts those promises, even as it struggles to make certain that its own community life witnesses to those promises. An ever-growing awareness of context fosters a spirituality committed to the values that once illuminated the life and ministry of Jesus.

Context and *promise* are at the heart of the spirituality of a congregation that shares the spirituality of God's reign. Examining a context in the light of God's promises is the starting point for all ministry that takes that reign seriously. It affects every aspect of a congregation's life: education, worship, even care for the members.

LEARNING AND THE REIGN OF GOD

As we noted, the letter to the Ephesians cited above reminded its first readers that the Christian community is not divided between energetic leaders and passive followers. The goal is a community in which everyone is developing a mature faith, a perspective that sees clearly the reality of the world and perceives the possibility of having a hand in reshaping it according to God's will.

The congregation is the primary place where individuals who identify with the spirituality of Jesus learn to do as he did: to read their world as it is, and as it might be. A congregation dedicated to making an impact on the world will see times of coming together as times for learning about that world.

But times of gathering are also opportunities for revisiting the story of Jesus and our ancestors in faith. These times are not for engaging in a blind repetition of what they did in their time, but for being reminded of what it means to act on behalf of God's reign, to be and to create signs and, when necessary, to resist the powers of death.

In the enterprise of growing in awareness of the world around us, the story of Jesus, and the way that story has been lived out by Christians ever since, everyone is both teacher and learner. All of us have experienced the world; all of us have profited from the way things are, and all of us have suffered from it. In hearing one another's stories, the congregation develops an awareness without which ministry is haphazard and probably irrelevant. Learning from one another's lives of faith, how the promise of God's reign has called us, how we have succeeded—and failed—to live as part of the story, the congregation becomes the context for growing the spirituality of Jesus in ways that make sense to twenty-first century Christians.

WORSHIP AND THE REIGN OF GOD

The congregation does not gather only to strengthen awareness of the world and how God's reign challenges it. Christians also gather to worship. But what does our worship look like in the light of the reign of God?

First, worship that takes God's reign seriously recognizes that the very act of coming together, breaking bread, and drinking wine in memory of Jesus can be not only a sign of God's reign but also an opportunity to experience what it is like to live in the *shalom* it promises. In order for that to be true, certain things must happen.

We must give up thinking about worship as a private affair between God and self. Unless our point of reference is the gathered community, worship will signify nothing except our own individual concerns. The whole point of congregational worship is the nature of the community that comes together. A gathering of worshipers preoccupied with their own private agendas, even their own private spirituality, falls far short of the community of *shalom* that a church at worship is meant to be.

Second, the internal life of the congregation must reflect the fundamental equality of the children of God that is a hallmark of God's reign. A congregation obsessed with hierarchy, with categories of influence or power, with making invidious distinctions between persons or groups can never reflect God's intentions for humankind. If worship is to be a sign of the promise of God's reign, then *how* the congregation lives and worships together will determine how it claims the spirituality of Jesus for its own life.

When a congregation succeeds in creating a community of mutual respect, then worship can be a joyous celebration of its own life and its hopes for the world. The needs and pains of its members and their neighbors can be brought into the heart of worship, to be offered to God along with all our gifts, to receive blessing and healing.

The possibilities of worship in the light of God's reign are never fulfilled more fully than when the shared Eucharistic meal becomes a genuine sign and vehicle of *communion* between those who have gathered to share it. Broken bread and poured-out wine become the powerful signs of the fundamental gestures of love and concern that are at the heart of Jesus' spirituality—and of those who would make it their own.

PREACHING AND THE REIGN OF GOD

In such a context of gathered worship, the sermon is an integral part of telling the story of Jesus and applying it to personal situations and the reality of the world we live in. In such worship, the sermon is not isolated from the rest of worship or from the congregation's life, but basic to it. The sermon is a primary means by which the story of Jesus is presented and proclaimed in such a way that it is both clear and inviting. It is an important source for reflection about how individuals might make the story their own. Good preaching that takes God's reign seriously is always contextual and always hopeful. It never fails to remind the congregation of the good news that brought them together in the first place.

Unlike many sermons with which Christians are all too familiar, preaching that takes God's reign seriously never attempts to tell its hearers what to do; rather, it explains the story of Jesus in ways that invite participation and response. This is sometimes described as a "circle of discourse." The sermon is usually open-ended and presupposes commentary and reflection on the part of its hearers, for whom it will ultimately be a kind of "raw material" for their own individual and shared reflection and action.

Preaching from the perspective of God's reign always reminds us of who we are: children of God and gifted with the Spirit. But it is not meant merely to make us "feel good."

Authentic preaching also invites and challenges us to make the story of Jesus our own and to live as agents of God's reign.

PASTORAL CARE AND THE REIGN OF GOD

The rampant individualism of contemporary culture in the United States has obscured the importance of the community experience for claiming the spirituality of Jesus. We are challenged to reclaim that dimension of Jesus' perspective in every aspect of our gathered life as a congregation. If it affects how we perceive our Christian education and our worship, it also has implications for how we undertake pastoral care.

If you asked most Christians in the United States what "pastoral care" means, they will probably focus on the spiritual comfort, advice, and counseling provided by clergy or other church professionals to individuals and families in times of crisis. As such, it is seen as a private activity that affects only the individuals actually engaged in it.

Pastoral care undertaken with reference to the reign of God begins from an entirely different supposition. It is the web of opportunities for being strengthened, comforted, and healed that are part of the congregation's life and available to any of its members who are in need of those resources. This does not mean that there will not be individuals, clergy or lay, with the specific gifts that make them good listeners and compassionate friends. In fact, from what Paul tells us about the gifts of the Spirit present in any community, we can assume that those gifts will be present.

But a congregation dedicated to God's reign will see pastoral care as part of every aspect of its life, and as part of the framework for strengthening its members in understanding, commitment, and compassion. It is not the special territory of a handful of professionals, but the very fabric of a congregation's life together.

The Gathered Church and God's Reign:
A Case Study

The marks of a congregation that understands its own life from the perspective of the reign of God are not hard to identify if we read the story of Jesus and his followers and set out to claim it for our own lives. But what would such a congregation be like? Case studies often help us to make concrete what would otherwise remain abstract. Their purpose is not to invite us to replicate them, but to learn from the experience of others what faithfulness looks like in a particular context in order to live more faithfully in our own. The story of one large and committed African American church in Los Angeles can serve as a study of the shape of faithfulness over the last decade in a troubled and divided community.

In April, 1992, a jury acquitted four Los Angeles police officers of beating an African American man named Rodney King, though the beating had been recorded on video. That film may well be the most-watched video in the history of the medium. Within hours of the acquittal, Los Angeles exploded in violence and entire neighborhoods were in flames. As the world watched in horror, years and decades of rage and frustration took out their fury on the city. Many for whom the "American dream" remains illusory were caught up in the anger and violence of the moment: African Americans wounded by racism and institutions that program them for failure; young Asians and Central Americans who had fled to a promised land that had not delivered on its promises; Americans of Mexican descent whose ancestors were in California long before it joined the United States, but who are still treated as if they are in exile; the grandchildren of the farmers who left the Midwest during the Great Depression and have yet to find a better life. These are the people of the margins, the ones who always seem to be left behind, left outside. In Los Angeles and its environs they number in the millions; yet for the most part life in the metropolis continues as if they do not matter.

When a troubled peace came at last to the streets of Los Angeles, it was probably due less to the soldiers and police than to the efforts of the city's churches. That effort was led by the Reverend Cecil Murray, pastor of the First African Methodist Episcopal Church, known as FAME.

The congregation was founded more than a century ago by a Georgia-born ex-slave who became a wealthy landowner and who made her home available for Black worshipers until she was able to purchase a site for the first church building. By the 1990s, FAME had become not only a worshiping community but a corporation. Today its active membership has reached 10,000 with a staff of 150, including administrators, youth workers, and more than 50 ministers and ministers-in-training. Sunday morning worship is at the heart of FAME's life. All services incorporate the traditional African American element known as call-and-response, in which the preacher's words are answered by assent from the congregation.

Pastor Murray is critical of the worship style often associated with African American Christianity, which he believes emphasizes emotional experience that has little effect on the way people live.[2] He is equally critical of the tradition of worship in most white churches, which tends to concentrate on a rational approach to God without taking into account the whole person. Murray advocates worship aimed at "the head, the heart, and the feet," satisfying both the emotional and intellectual need for God, and also directing worshipers into creative confrontation with the world.

Those who are part of FAME (mostly African American, but with a scattered 1 to 2 percent of other ethnic groups) drive from all over the Los Angeles area to participate in its life.

---

[2]Quotes and viewpoints from the Reverend Cecil Murray are from a personal interview with him.

Their involvement does not end with the conclusion of the Sunday service; those who request formal membership are asked to join one of the dozens of task forces that address the enormous needs of the community at a time of great social conflict and economic misery. The congregation understands the rhythm of *gathering and scattering,* noting in a brochure that "we come in to worship to go out to serve." In Pastor Murray's words, the fullness of Christian faith "baptizes both the individual and the environment." The church is not concerned with either individual or social salvation, but with both simultaneously. The good news of God's reign impels the Christian community, as God's Word-made-flesh in the here and now, to recognize itself as the extension of God's love in the world. The church responds to immediate human needs, but also teaches individuals to take responsibility for themselves. Christ's good news calls the church to nothing less than the healing of a broken world.

FAME task forces provide legal counseling, tutoring, and support for persons suffering from cancer and AIDS; they work with homeless people (the church houses several hundred homeless people every night); and they address problems of alcohol and drug abuse, all of which their pastor calls "a kaleidoscope of the community of need."

FAME has earned a well-deserved reputation for taking risks. Its mission, Murray says, is to "take up the slack" where other congregations are put off by fear or controversy. The congregation works extensively with neighborhood gangs, serving as a bridge and seeking to prevent violence.

FAME's presence in the community is multifaceted. It has overseen the construction of housing worth tens of millions of dollars, including apartments for disabled people. It started a community-based school and works with hundreds of at-risk youth, using volunteers drawn almost entirely from the church's own members.

Following the 1992 unrest, FAME launched a major economic program aimed at addressing the conditions of chronic poverty and unemployment that have plagued African Americans. "FAME Renaissance," founded "to enhance business and economic development for our community," sought to provide both entrepreneurial expertise and resources for new business ventures; offered training in business skills; and made micro-loans. Operating costs were borne by the congregation, but hundreds of corporations also contributed to the program. In its first year alone, FAME Renaissance provided more than two thousand jobs to members of its community.

How can one congregation grow to exercise such a role in the community? Pastor Murray identifies three factors. One is that FAME has not shunned publicity. Two, FAME attracts people from the entire spectrum of the African American population of Los Angeles. Its membership includes celebrities and the affluent as well as welfare recipients, "the gifted and the grass-roots," because the congregation has communicated its belief that *both have important gifts the church needs.* Three, FAME is responding to the spiritual hunger it sees in Americans as our country has become what Murray describes as "a mean nation."

FAME understands that the religious community alone cannot solve the problems of a country with millions of unskilled homeless people. Murray says, "We need a national agenda with a simple wish list, tied to askings from corporations, government, and other funding sources." But if the churches cannot solve the problem alone, they can surely provide the leadership to awaken the national conscience and begin to acknowledge the deep longing for a different kind of world that still lies buried in the human heart. The church, Murray believes, is called to create a setting where "it is all right to feel again, to believe again, to hope again." This requires conversion to a vision that affirms the value of our diversity. "The greatest challenge facing us," Murray says, "is how to get along with each other."

After the 1992 Los Angeles uprising, FAME commissioned artist George Yapes to create a mural at the church's west entrance that would embody the church's heritage as it gives birth to new life. In Yapes's painting, a male African figure represents Joseph blessing the son Jesus. A Black Madonna blesses her daughter, the mind of the people. The design also includes the phoenix, a sign of rebirth, and the Egyptian sacred scarab, an African symbol of resurrection. A FAME brochure describes it as being set against the background of south central Los Angeles in flames. Beneath it is this caption: "We at FAME are determined to make the Word of God's Peace and Justice become flesh."

Surely that is a fitting slogan for any congregation steeped in the story and the spirituality of Jesus and God's reign.

Toward the Future

As the old millennium gave way to the new, one of the noteworthy phenomena of American culture was the emergence of an entirely new format of popular entertainment: so-called "reality TV." Of course, this new genre makes use of the same technology that shapes other television programming. There are producers and directors, camera crews, and a small army of support personnel; and although "reality TV" does not respond to a written script, the finished product is very much dependent on the process of editing, weeding out those parts of "reality" that are not suitable for television viewing.

Some programming is based on what happens when ordinary people are placed in a setting that tries to recreate an earlier period in history: an English family spends weeks in a house that replicates a 1900 house; American families are challenged to relive the Montana frontier. Part of the "entertainment" is intended to come from observing how they cope, and fail to cope, with conditions that are not only difficult but also different. (Of course, the difficulty lies in the fact that in 1900 London or on the American frontier, everyone else was living in similar conditions and had not experienced the modern world.)

Still other "reality TV" programs focus on the dynamics of one family, or on single persons intent on finding their perfect mates, or on individuals verbally attacking each other for real or supposed affronts, or on victims enduring tongue-lashings disguised as "advice" by so-called "professionals." The central characters at the heart of these programs are not stars, but real human beings, who for reasons known only to themselves are willing to become vulnerable, to air their grievances, and perhaps to suffer humiliation for a television audience.

Perhaps the most popular of all is the *Survivor* series in which small groups of carefully selected individuals live in increasingly difficult settings and take on the challenge of forming communities. Then they compete as teams against each other, and finally vote periodically on the elimination of one of their number. The motivation for the competition is a huge monetary prize for the winner.

Survivor differs from earlier types of TV competitions in several important ways. First, contestants are not merely demonstrating their ability to recall facts or to perform stunts involving questionable skill or significance, like the quiz shows of an earlier generation. They must actually live together in community under rigorous conditions, depending on one another's ingenuity, prowess, and skill for food and shelter. We would expect such behavior to foster a high degree of cooperation, and indeed it does. But the "rules of the game" decree that the weakest members of the group—those less skilled, wise, or pleasant to be around—are "killed off" in a ruthless mimicking of what is claimed to be a demonstration of "survival of the fittest."

But victory—surviving to win the prize given at the end of the program—demands more than just ruthlessness and individual strengths. It also inevitably involves forming tactical alliances with others in order to "pick off" the weakest members of the groups and limit the playing field. And, of course, the audience gets involved in the drama of the competition, cheering on both the teamwork and the betrayals, the victories and the humiliations. Professor Karal Ann Marling calls such programming "mean TV," and she is certainly right. Devotees of such programs, she writes, are:

> perpetual onlookers to their own lives, thanks to TV: they have no responsibility for the yelling and the bloodshed—no stake in the mayhem, which makes it all too easy to enjoy wickedness from a distance. Merely watching things happen absolves the viewer of any responsibility for them. Those are somebody else's troubles on the screen, and, as such, of no real consequence.[1]

The medium itself is not the villain in the emergence of "mean TV." As the most popular medium in the United States for both information and entertainment, television is, nevertheless, a mirror of the values that shape us as a people. What does "reality TV" invite us to believe, and how does it give us permission, even urge us, to act?

Certainly it assumes that the natural human condition is the *individual* in all his or her solitude. The rules of the game decree that there can be only one winner at the end. This, in turn, determines how we are to view all relationships, all allegiances to other individuals or groups, and all communities. They are in the end *strategic, tactical commitments* made in order to achieve what remains an individual goal. Even intimate relationships do not ultimately transcend the person; the point is not the well-being of the other but of oneself. They are arrangements of convenience for the

---

[1]Karal Ann Marling, "They Want Their Mean TV," *The New York Times*, 26 May 2002, sec. 2: 1, 32–33.

satisfaction of the individual's needs, wishes, or desires; and in the end, the needs and well-being of anyone else are irrelevant. Loyalty to any other individual, family, or group is a means to an end which must finally be personal and private.

Second, the individual's happiness is understood in material terms. (We must remember that "the pursuit of happiness" is enshrined in the Declaration of Independence as one of the most basic human rights to which human beings are entitled, along with our life and our liberty.) Most people in the United States do not measure happiness in relationships, memories, or creativity; we are much more likely to measure it by more tangible means, and above all by the accumulation of wealth and what wealth buys. Indeed, those aspects of human culture that might be thought to stand outside the scale of material value—such as art, ability, even relationships—can be turned into commodities with a price tag or instruments of achieving wealth. Satisfying our most basic human needs for food, shelter, clothing, and mobility can be converted, if we choose, into symbols and instruments of success: *how, where, and what we eat, where we live and in what kind of dwelling, how we dress and the price tags on our clothing, how we travel and in what kind of vehicle.* These can become signs of winning in the contest of life, so that possessing them becomes part of the competition, for which no price is too high to pay.

Accepting the assumptions that this is an appropriate way to seek and find happiness keeps our economy running at its best level. Business in a culture like ours is geared not to human need, but to human desires. Those desires, in turn, are honed and refined by the symbols of success that appear to be directly related to pursuing and finding happiness. A vast advertising industry keeps busy persuading United States consumers (and those around the world who would mimic us) that our lives will be improved and transformed if only we purchase whatever product is currently in fashion as carrying the hallmark of success. Driving a particular car, wearing particular clothing, even wearing a particular (expensive) perfume will define us as "successful" in the only way that matters, which in turn will bring us satisfaction and happiness.

The engine that drives relationships among human beings in a society like ours is *competition.* "Winning," as the old adage goes, "isn't everything; it's the only thing." Life itself becomes a race or a contest in which each individual is ranged against every other. The family becomes a contest for the attention of a parent; a marriage is a "battle of wills;" the workplace is "a rat race"; competition between nations is often conceived as a war, whether or not conventional weapons are involved. The United States, we are told, is in a war to guarantee itself the fuel it needs to maintain its current lifestyle, whatever the consequences to other peoples or, for that matter, to the planet.

It is important to notice how we have been taught to describe the television programming that affirms these values: "reality TV." In other words, in spite of the obvious artifice of editing, as well as the constant presence of the crews and equipment that make it possible, we are persuaded that what we are viewing is "reality"—"the way things are."

Not only does the image of life projected by this genre of programming claim to be "the way things are"; it is assumed that this portrays an *unchangeable* reality, as if individualism and competition were somehow written into the very fabric of the universe. Indeed, for several hundred years, a number of thinkers have claimed precisely that: The goal of creation is our individual happiness, probably measured in entirely material terms (such as the million dollars that winners on *Survivor* receive). Striving for our own fulfillment means inevitably struggling against, and defeating, others. The implication is clear: this is the way of the world, and it shapes our destiny. Our well-being depends on how successfully we conform ourselves to it. No culture in the world has been as effectively shaped by that perspective as our own has. The value placed on the "rugged individual," the definition of happiness in material terms, and the acceptance of a competitive spirit say a great deal about who we are as a people.

And yet a critical eye toward the national soul raises some troubling questions. Individualism has its limits. Persons who trust no one and claim to need no one overlook the facts of life that guarantee times when we do indeed need one another. Furthermore, the testimony of the human family around the world is that individualism inevitably overlooks some human traits, such as loyalty, compassion, and selfless love. A broader perspective would suggest that a more authentic way of living as human beings would seem to be *interdependence,* a concept for which our culture makes little allowance.

There are also serious problems with defining happiness in terms of what we are able to accumulate. The fundamental contradiction is based on the fact that the planet on which we depend for our survival has only finite resources. If everyone has the right to seek—and find—happiness, but some take the lion's share of those resources on which that happiness depends, inevitably most of us will be shortchanged. Our basic right to happiness will evaporate into unfulfilled wishes.

Certainly there are basic human needs without which we live in misery. But perhaps happiness is not measured best in how much we can amass in excess of what we really need, but in other terms altogether. Down through the ages, human history suggests that there are, in fact, other dimensions to happiness and fulfillment than the accumulation of possessions and the status that goes with them. These include serving God's will and purposes, the joys of enduring relationships, the bonds between the generations, commitment to purposes greater than ourselves, the possibility of celebration, and the outpouring of human creativity.

We must also wonder if the assumption that human beings take priority over the rest of creation is an accurate reading of "the way things are." Certainly humankind can manipulate and destroy our global homeland if we choose; the evidence is all around us. What we may not always notice, however, is that such arrogance breeds consequences. The effects of global warming affect human beings and society, as well as play havoc with the delicate balance of life, which includes all living species and of which humans are only a part. If there is no water for agriculture, if farmland becomes desert, if the rainforests are destroyed, if pristine environments are trampled in the endless search for more oil, the consequences will be global and individual.

We should also take a hard look at whether competition is, in fact, the best engine for promoting the welfare of individuals and peoples. Winning is pleasurable, as any athlete or investor knows. But losing is not. Losing means anxiety, fear, depression, and perhaps, if the stakes are high enough, misery or death. The widespread poverty that mars the Earth's human landscape is a reminder that where there are winners, losers also exist in a world where losing can be fatal.

Even in a society as prosperous as our own, in which the drive for success energizes day-and-night competition, the plight of those who do not succeed has become increasingly evident. A generation ago, homelessness was unknown in America. Now we have become accustomed to the incredible statistics that assure us that the number of homeless people in our streets has risen to the millions. In the same way, the great number of individuals, often young and mostly members of ethnic minorities, who are currently imprisoned mocks the equality of opportunity—the "level playing field"—our culture claims to provide for the competitive game of economics. Indeed, the so-called "correctional industry," which has very little to do with correction but a great deal to do with losing, has blossomed and flourished in recent decades.

These are powerful signs, if any were needed, that our culture has been built on core values that need to be challenged or tempered. And indeed, our culture is being challenged in some powerful, dramatic, and painful ways to re-examine its central assumptions. Ironically, the same medium that has offered us what claims to be "reality TV" has also been instrumental in raising questions. It has proven to be an extraordinary means of communicating events and movements that call into question the individuality, materialism, and competition at the heart of our culture. Following are several such watershed markers from the many that could be chosen:

The AIDS epidemic. The mysterious epidemic of Acquired Immune Deficiency Syndrome, or AIDS, first shocked people in the early 1980s. Within a short time, thousands had been infected and were dying. What had appeared at first to be a disease largely limited to the gay community was, in fact, an international plague of vast proportions, infecting millions of all ages. For the first time in nearly a century, Americans experienced the deaths of large numbers of young persons as medical professionals watched helplessly.

Although medical advances in the past decade have extended the life expectancy of those infected with AIDS who are able to afford the exorbitant treatment costs, those individuals who know or who are caring for AIDS sufferers have a new awareness of mortality and human dependence. Against such a backdrop of suffering and loss, the charms of the consumer culture seem much less attractive. Responding to the AIDS pandemic has caused many to question the extreme individualism in which lives have been shaped. At the same time, the possibility of a meaningful life in the face of so much death becomes a challenging question.

The life and death of Diana, Princess of Wales. When Lady Diana Spencer married the heir to the British throne, people all over the world were captivated by what seemed to be the real-life version of a romance novel. Diana epitomized the values of a culture captivated by glamour and success. But her real-life suffering, culminating in a divorce, transformed both Diana and her admiring public. Always personable, she became the sought-after champion of others who were suffering. She freely offered her time on behalf of charities dedicated to victims of AIDS, land mines, and others, becoming a symbol of compassion that was just the opposite of the glamorous success she had once represented. Her untimely death in an automobile accident evinced a planetary outpouring of grief never before seen. In cities around the world, strangers waited in line for hours to sign memorial booklets and to leave offerings of flowers. Once again, death had stripped away the fairy-tale veneer of what had once seemed the perfectly successful life

Globalization and the Internet. The international outpouring of sorrow at Diana's death underscores one of the most dramatic developments of the end of the twentieth century: the phenomenon of globalization, which continues to shape the new millennium.

More than a generation has passed since Marshall McLuhan first introduced us to the concept of the *global village*. In the early 1960s he began talking about communication. As soon as we heard what he had to say, we recognized instinctively that he was right: the distances that separated us were growing smaller and smaller. Since McLuhan's time, mobile phones, faxes, and the Internet have made communication around the world an almost instantaneous process.

But globalization does not refer only to communication. It is used most frequently to describe the "new economic order" that is being proposed as the inevitable course of history, in which traditional boundaries are ignored in favor of a "free market." To a large degree, this is happening. So we wear sneakers stitched in Indonesia, shirts sewn in Singapore, watch televisions put together in Mexico, and drive cars made in Canada by companies with Japanese names. The shapers of this new global economy are what we have learned to call "multinational corporations" because they seem to exist everywhere and really belong nowhere; and the giant international agencies, such as the World Bank and the International Monetary Fund, which use economic pressure to create conditions in other countries that are good for investment.

This "new economic order" is intended to produce a kind of global division of labor in which industry is concentrated in poor countries, while rich countries deal more in the management of information. This, it is believed, will create a "trickle-down" prosperity: jobs created in poor countries will turn millions into consumers, who can then buy what *they* have made and *we* are selling. It sounds so good to some that our leaders assure us it is inevitable. Globalization, they tell us, is not something created, maintained, and regulated by human hands and minds, but something with its own identity and life that follows not human but "natural" laws, no longer stoppable, marching forward to unseen goals, and inviting us to follow where we cannot yet see. Both immensely attractive to some and enormously frightening to others, this progression demands loyalty and commitment, including the possibility that many will be called on to suffer for the sake of a prosperity in which they will never share.

But what is the *reality* of globalization? Based as it is on competition and consumption, it inevitably creates winners and losers. In 1960, the richest 20 percent of the world's population controlled 30 times the wealth of the poorest 30 percent. By 2000, the richest 20 percent controlled 74 times the wealth of the poorest 30 percent. Faith in the inevitability and rightness of globalization is becoming harder to maintain as the gap between rich and poor widens around the world and in every country, including the United States.

Another unforeseen side effect of this "inevitable reality" is that the conditions for a global economy weaken or destroy the protection of the natural environment and the rights of workers, such as minimum wage and health and retirement benefits. In effect, the whole world is suffering, as huge amounts of cheap food mass-produced in the rich countries using the technology of agribusiness overwhelms small farmers in poor countries, drives them off the land and into the cities, where there is no work. Meanwhile, the service of the international debt carried by poor nations, contracted a generation ago and repaid many times in interest, continues to leave impoverished countries powerless to control their own future. Interest payments eat into education budgets, health care budgets, and retirement plans. Even working families can no longer care for their children. In Costa Rica, a country of 3 million that once took pride in having one of the most humane levels of education and health care in Latin America, 110,000 children are now working in the streets. We might well ask if globalization is not a kind of idol, a false deity that requires human sacrifice, above all the sacrifice of the poor, the old, and the young. They are the masses who are excluded, excluded when people talk about the benefits of the new global economy and excluded from meaningful work, from the possibility of a living income, from the option of living to old age.

Ironically, just when economic globalization is creating an ever wider gap between those who prosper from the system and those who are its victims, the Internet and other modern means of communication make the opposing poles of the new reality far more evident. Indeed, the poor must travel past the shops crammed with consumer goods to reach the shantytowns they call home. Often they survive by cleaning the homes, tending the children, or washing the luxury cars of the wealthy. A form of "unreality TV"—the ever-present soap operas that form the regular entertainment of millions of the poor around the world—depict the glamorous life of the successful minority whose lives could not be farther removed from those of the millions of viewers who envy them. People on both sides of the great divide between rich and poor are peering uneasily into the vast spaces that have opened between them. Many have begun to wonder if, in fact, this is the best of which humankind is capable.

Drugs and the failed war. A defining characteristic of the global consumer culture that has shaped the last decades of the old millennium and intrudes on the new one is the emergence of international drug trafficking, designed to meet the incessant demands for narcotics, especially in the wealthier nations. Entire regional economies have been dedicated to the production of opium and heroin, with the inevitable participation of international criminal organizations and terrorist regimes. In a number of Asian and Latin American countries, the supply of drugs to the developed world has created a culture of crime, violence, and early death that mimics the conditions under which the drugs are used and sold in the United States and other wealthy countries. Expensive campaigns to eradicate the crops, stop the importing of drugs, and seek out those responsible have been costly and disastrous failures. Meanwhile, many neighborhoods of American cities have become killing fields. We might well consider the drug trade as an example of the reality of globalization, and its perpetrators a type of "multinational corporation," albeit an illegal one.

The one facet of the campaign against drugs that is almost never seriously addressed is the question of why so many individuals, especially the young, find themselves ensnared in the complex system that produces and sells drugs. Most of the crimes committed in this country are directly or indirectly related to drugs; yet few ask who are the drug users and the drug dealers, and what are the circumstances that have brought them to a way of life that will certainly kill them. What level of despair, what failure of possibility would impel people to opt for death rather than life?

September 11, 2001. The terrorist attacks on the Pentagon and the World Trade Center on September 11, 2001, marked a watershed moment for all Americans. Powerful emotions were unleashed, including profound fear and a thirst for revenge. But the terrible events of that day also raised deep questions. Many found themselves wondering about the nature of security and where it might be found. Others discovered the limits of individualism, as they felt the terrible grief of that day. Still others asked if the motivating rage behind such terrorism is a by-product of global injustice. Many longed for a community—a community of trust, support, and care for one another.

The Reign of God in the New Millennium

And so, in the months and years that have followed September 11, 2001, we have arrived at the place at which this book began—longing for a framework in which to explore the possibility of faith and to seek meaning in this strange new world in which no one feels entirely at home. We are yearning for a place to stand, a stable center from which to ask the difficult questions and seek a way to live fully.

A twenty-first century spirituality. This book has set out a way of approaching and claiming the story of Jesus as the framework of a spirituality for times like these and for people like ourselves. Perhaps the ways twenty-first century Christians make the story their own and retell it in the shaping of their lives will not look exactly like the Christian spirituality of other times and places. Given the contextual way in which the story has always been claimed, we should not be surprised by this. Whatever its form, the story will continue to rely on our claiming it in such a way that it awakens hope.

The promises of the reign of God will be brought squarely into engagement with the challenging realities of "the world as it is." But the purpose of the story is not to help us accept the world as it is. Rather, the story will help us recognize what needs to change; and by awakening our hope, it will give us resources for becoming instruments of change. "New life" is not simply a pious phrase, but the description of the hope that motivates us as we live out Jesus' story in our own circumstances.

A truly twenty-first century spirituality will surely be deeply rooted in the experience of the Christian *community*, as a way of countering the bankrupt individualism and competition that pervades our popular culture. The twenty centuries of Christian history that form our heritage amply demonstrate just how essential the community of faith is for claiming fully the story of Jesus and making it our own story. The experience of telling and living the story together can provide a secure framework for challenging the myths that poison our culture. There is no element of Christian faith that is more *countercultural* with reference to the dominant American culture of individualism, consumerism, and competition than the insistence that our true humanity only becomes clear as we embrace, and are embraced by, a community of others. Those *others* who make up the body of Christ for us are not our adversaries in some cosmic competition; they are our sisters and brothers in a global project: finding, creating, and becoming signs of God's own reign, the vision of *shalom* that has always been our true destiny.

The Christian community that takes *shalom* seriously, both as a mark of its own life and a hope for the world, will value the *diversity* of others in ways the church has not always honored. Most of us no longer live in villages surrounded by friends and family remarkably like us; we live in more complex settings made up of people from around the world. If the church is to be a sign of the peace for which the world longs, its life will mirror that diversity; and it will respect human differences and incorporate them into its own life in creative ways. Mindful of Paul's insistence that each of its members has gifts to be used on behalf of God's reign, the church will claim a spirituality for the new millennium that will be attentive to those gifts and how each of us can be agents of *shalom*.

For twenty-first century Christians, the experience of community will almost certainly be focused on the experience of *worship,* understood not as a private act between the individual and God, but as an opportunity to forget ourselves in the praise of the Holy that lies behind and beyond all life. Genuine worship brings clarity of vision and focuses our hope. It lifts our hearts beyond our own private needs and places those needs in the context of a much larger perspective, as wide as the planet on which we live.

A community of Christians that truly honors diversity will express spirituality in ways that reflect the experience of peoples from around the world. While it will be clear in its faithfulness to the story of Jesus and the promise of the reign of God at the heart of his story, it will also be open to the wisdom and insight of other traditions. The symbolism of breaking bread together is rooted in the gesture of Jesus at his last supper. This will be interpreted as a radically inviting gesture, offering the possibility of shared life to those both inside and beyond the community of faith, and encompassing God's promise of abundance for humankind and for the Earth.

This sensitivity finds regular expression in the worship of Grace Cathedral, an Episcopal church in San Francisco. When the bread is broken in the Eucharist, the congregation prays:

> We break this bread for those who journey the way of the Hindus, for those who follow the path of the Buddha, for our sisters and brothers of Islam, and for the Jewish People from whom we come. We break this bread for the earth we have wasted, for those who have no bread, and for our ourselves in our brokenness.

In this way, they affirm that the *shalom* of sharing bread and drinking wine together does not apply only to the congregation but also to the world community, to the wounded planet, and to each of us in our own need and pain.

The attitude that shapes such an open and welcoming spirituality is a response to the awareness that the God who gave us the dream of *shalom*, who speaks to us through the story of Jesus and his followers and our own living of that story, nevertheless remains partially hidden from us. No revelation given to mere mortals can encompass the totality of the holy mystery to whom the scriptures give the name of *God*. Elements of the Christian story make that point but have not always been noticed, and it is past time to reclaim them.

Moving among the cosmopolitan peoples of the Roman Empire, Paul never failed to seize the opportunity to share the story of Jesus with anyone who would listen. But he also knew well that the God who spoke to him through the story of Jesus had already spoken in other ways, not only to his own people the Jews, but also through the many traditions that jostled one another in the marketplace and on street corners. Living as we do in a world similar to Paul's, where a myriad of beliefs call out for our attention, living the story of Jesus and his followers might well move us to talk with people formed in those traditions, not only to explain how we have discovered the vision of *shalom* in a way that gives meaning and purpose to our life but also to hear how that vision has been spoken in other times and places. In discovering how people of other traditions have laid claim to that promise, we might find insights and practices that will help us claim the story of Jesus in ways that make sense to us.

The Christian story through the ages includes many people who grasped a part of the mysterious nature of the God who spoke through Jesus, and they dedicated their lives to deeper communion with that holy Mystery. We call them *mystics* because, in their prayer and meditation, their rigorous commitment and the practices by which they lived their commitment, they saw how deep and mysterious is the holy God who speaks to us through stories and signs.

Often the wider church has ignored or even mistreated the mystics, because their vision of God spills "outside the lines" and passes beyond the everyday language with which we ordinarily speak. Transformed by the vision of the God behind the promises, they sometimes convey their insight in silence, relying on the sign of their own lives rather than anything they say or write—though they were and are often driven to communicate their experience in writing for those who have not shared it.

A twenty-first century spirituality will no doubt reclaim the experience of the mystics of earlier times as another resource for knowing the One whose dream we share. The community of faith can be a context for discovering and exploring the rich diversity of wisdom and experience that the mystics of our own and other traditions offer us.

The church that is welcoming enough to offer a truly twenty-first century Christianity will make room for those at all levels of engagement with the story it tells. The carefully crafted summaries of what Christians believe—the Creeds, Catechisms, and other documents by which people of faith in times past put their beliefs into words—are important parts of the story of the church in other times. They deserve our attention and respect. But in the new millennium, faith will much more likely be defined by stories than by creeds born in academic debate or political infighting. The concerns that shaped those documents are probably not ours; all too often, they were composed in the heat of argument, to attack those whose perceptions of the Christian story and of God were different. In other words, they were often meant not only to *welcome* and *include* those who shared a common point of view, but also to *reproach* and *exclude* those who disagreed on one point or another.

Of course, how we understand the story of Jesus and his followers matters. Misreadings of that story have had serious consequences in the world. For example, individuals and groups have used the contexts of our ancestors in faith to argue for slavery, racial superiority, or war, even though the teaching of Jesus makes such an interpretation nearly impossible. But a twenty-first century spirituality that begins from the story of Jesus will draw people from many backgrounds and traditions—and from no religion at all. Nurturing that spirituality within the community of faith means openness to distinct points of view, and the comfortable acceptance of a spirit of questioning and dialogue, rather than debate and rigid definitions. Stories by their very nature are open and invite conversation; claiming and living a story will be more likely to produce diversity than uniformity.

A Case Study

What would a congregation that worked to put Jesus' story into practice look like? All Saints' Episcopal Church is an old congregation located in the Highland Park area of Los Angeles. When its members approached their current pastor, the Reverend William Leeson, about coming to work at All Saints', he told them that if he accepted their call, they would begin a new direction in ministry.[2] It was clear that only a radical change would enable the parish to survive. On his first Sunday in 1988, only about twenty of its sixty members attended the worship service.

Bill Leeson knew something about the neighborhood surrounding the church. Nearby areas had become home to a large number of gay and lesbian individuals; there was also a sizable Filipino population; and eighty-five percent of the neighborhood was Spanish-speaking. If he were to consider accepting All Saints' call, he told them, he would focus on ministering to those three groups; and, in time, they would become the primary constituents of the parish. To his surprise, the congregation agreed.

Highland Park is a poor neighborhood that feels intensely every downturn in the city's economy. While most residents have some kind of work, many are day-laborers, working as house cleaners or gardeners, while others work in small

---

[2]Information about and quotes from the Reverend William Leeson are from a personal interview with him.

workshops assembling clothing. Extended families often share cramped houses or apartments, and homeless people have slept on the church's grounds for months at a time. Gunshots sometimes shatter the night stillness.

Many of the Highland Park families came to the United States, some of them illegally, to escape war and misery. They bear hard and painful memories, and the scars of fear and loss. Within a few years after Leeson became the pastor, many of the original members had died, while others moved away from the steadily declining neighborhood. Ministry did change.

On a spring Saturday, a visitor to the church might observe the parish providing space for a citizenship examination, while a group of volunteers prepares bags of food obtained at low cost from the Regional Food Bank, or at no cost from local supermarkets. Volunteers come from several local churches. Each week more than a thousand packages of food are distributed; no one is refused.

Meanwhile, in another part of the parish house, volunteers from the congregation are opening El Ropero ("The Clothes Closet"), where clothing collected from all over Los Angeles is sold at fifty cents per large bag. Proceeds help support the food bank. A separate AIDS pantry is one of the key elements of All Saints' ministry to those who are suffering from AIDS. On that same Saturday, thirty grade-school girls are on a field trip to the Los Angeles Zoo; the pastor is teaching a class of Spanish-speaking children the Lord's Prayer and reviewing the life of Jesus; volunteers are preparing for Sunday worship; and the auditorium is being readied for a Latino Youth Dance.

A simple A-frame church is the center of the congregation's life. An enormous free-hanging crucifix, an abstract sculpture of Christ fashioned from brass wire, dominates it. Pale green, yellow, and white banners stretch from floor to ceiling behind the altar. The choir loft in the rear of the church receives bright sunlight through a large window bearing the stylized design of a sunburst.

Sunday morning worship is mindful of the diverse character of the congregation. Worship in English sometimes includes elements of the service in Tagalog for the Filipino members. Music comes from the Episcopal Church's official hymnal, but also from the songs of the charismatic renewal movement. A synthesizer provides the sounds of an organ, and guitars and other instruments regularly join in.

Sunday morning is the primary time when All Saints' congregation encounters the story of God's reign. Members are no strangers to persecution or vulnerability. Many gay and lesbian members have come to All Saints' after bitter experiences of rejection at other churches. Some have grieved the deaths of loved ones from AIDS; others are infected with HIV or are dying from the disease themselves. Immigrant members have faced an uncertain future and the mindless cruelty of individuals and institutions who hold the power of life and death over them. Now they are living in a strange country where they may not understand or be understood. Many live in terror of being returned to their native land and have often felt faceless, nameless, voiceless, hopeless.

The good news proclaimed at All Saints addresses the lives of the church's people with immediacy and directness, in the idiom of its neighbors and in response to their needs. Three chapels serve as places of prayer, each with a bank of candles to be lit. The first has a statue of the Virgin Mary and Jesus. The second is dedicated to Our Lady of Guadalupe, and is much loved by the Latino members of the congregation. The third is the AIDS chapel, where a candle burns continually in memory of those who have died, and in prayer for those with HIV and AIDS, their caregivers, and those engaged in research. The style of preaching and teaching at All Saints' is straightforward and simple: God wills good for humankind; Christ came to proclaim that divine love and to show it through his life, death, and resurrection; Christ remains a personal and present Savior to be sought for comfort and healing; and that same Christ invites us to share his ministry of loving service.

At the Spanish service, there are rarely enough seats for the congregation. Music is lively and spirited, and the church is filled with people of all ages, usually in large family groups. Asked why they choose to attend the church, people note the warmth and sense of personal welcome they feel: "They know me by name," one said. Another reason is the opportunity provided for participation in worship and in service to the community. One identified All Saints' as "the church that helps people."

Indeed, one of the most striking facts about All Saints' Church is the members' level of involvement. Many of them have no previous experience in administration or organizing skills. One of its members, who joined the church in 1920 and remained active for more than seventy years, stayed on when most of the previous members of the church moved away. She found the intimacy and warmth of the congregation to be more attractive than any alternative available to her.

To Leeson, All Saints' is a "savory stew" to which new spices are constantly being added. "The task," he says, "is to forge a coalition which celebrates diversity and still has unity." He sees the church as open and welcoming to all individuals, ready to accept and celebrate them as they are. Tolerance rests on the recognition that different groups play important roles in the congregation's life. Tensions between groups perceived in impersonal terms are defused when they get to know one another, share a common vision, and work together on behalf of that vision.

All Saints' is a "walk-in" church; most members live in its neighborhood. The focus of its life and ministry is inevitably at the local level. In spite of the complexity of the congregation, the problems it confronts, and the maze of networks and programs essential to its functioning, its message is simple. The good news takes on life in the church community as members and friends gather week by week. As the children learn in their classes, "Christ wants to make the world a friendlier place." Or as the stark words read on the kneeling cushion in the AIDS Chapel: "Love one another."

Spirituality for the Twenty-first Century: A New Generation

It may be that the events of September 11, 2001, will be the defining moment for the generation that has come of age in the shadow of the new millennium, just as the assassination of John F. Kennedy and the Vietnam War defined the "Baby Boomer" generation of their parents.

Young adults take for granted many of the innovations that still seem strange to their elders. They have grown up with a sense of the global community, fostered by ever-present technology and a lifetime of communicating via cell phones, faxes, and the Internet. Wherever they live, they encounter diversity and difference to a degree unknown to earlier generations. But often they have had few opportunities for community, few stories to claim as their own, few resources for exploring the mystery at the heart of life and the world. Many are the children of divorce who have no clear sense of home. Many have almost no coherent knowledge of the Christian story or any other religious tradition.

Popular cultures that shape the generation born toward the end of the last century reveal a deep spiritual hunger and an attraction to the images and symbols of religion, but little in the way of story or content. There are overtones of anger, even rage, at the injustice that continues to mar our common history. There is a profound awareness of the fragility of life, of the vulnerability of being human, and a pervasive irony that is more comfortable with ambiguity than dogma. There is a winsome sadness at the way the Earth has been damaged by human greed. The cultures of the post-"Baby Boomer" generations shape *seekers* who are eager for dialogue, open to discovery, ready to be engaged by a vision that gives them purpose, tolerant of differences and doubt, mistrustful of certainty, and scornful of hypocrisy. Where on Earth are they to turn?

A congregation that has been shaped by the story of Jesus and that fosters his spirituality, that has responded to the promises of the reign of God and claimed *shalom* as the heart of its life together, can be a welcome framework for a twenty-first century spiritual quest.

In the experience of community, in claiming the story of Jesus as our own story, twenty-first century Christians can be transformed by baptism and nurtured by the Eucharist to become part of that story. We can claim a new identity and shape our life together as a sign of the hope that *shalom* continues to offer to every generation. We can become people of God's reign, calling into question the individualism, the materialism and greed, and the competition that are so readily accepted as the best our culture has to offer. We can place ourselves at the intersection between the pain and misery of the world, and the promise of the reign of God.

In that experience, hope is born again for a new generation. The promise of God's reign takes flesh among us.

Questions for Individual Reflection and Group Discussion

CHAPTER 1: *The Spirituality of Jesus*

1. What does "spirituality" mean to you?
2. Have you ever thought of the gospel in terms of the "reign of God"? How do you respond to this approach?
3. The author asserts that if we understand the "reign of God" as Jesus spoke of it, our freedom is not destroyed but affirmed. Do you agree? Why or why not?
4. How is the idea of *covenant* reflected in your understanding of God?
5. What does *shalom* mean to you? Does it help shape your spiritual life? If so, how?
6. The author writes, "The spirituality of Jesus and his people was a constant looking backward in order to look forward in hope." Do you recall memories that give you hope for the future?
7. Are you aware of "signs of the reign of God" in your own life? If so, what are some of them? Have they changed your relationship with God? If so, how?

CHAPTER 2: *Spirituality in Context*

1. Does understanding "signs of the reign of God" in Jesus' life and ministry help you as you think about "miracles"?

2. The author suggests that in any given context, "we do not experience the fullness of God's reign but rather signs and clues." Do you agree? How would this awareness affect your understanding of God?

3. According to the author, "the circumstances of our life...become the raw material of our life with God." What does this mean to you?

4. Have you ever experienced feelings like those of the writer of Psalm 137 (quoted in this chapter)? How was your faith affected by that experience?

5. "Stories lead to hope." Are there stories that are especially important to you in keeping hope alive? If so, what are they?

6. What are some moments in your life of "extreme tension between the way things are" and the way God wills them to be? Are there signs of God's reign that you encounter at such moments? If so, what are they?

CHAPTER 3: *Story and Community*

1. What does the phrase "body of Christ" mean to you?

2. The author states that the story of Jesus changed the priorities, values, and behavior of those who first heard it. Do you agree? Can the story of Jesus still have that effect?

3. The first Christians were known as "followers of 'The Way'." Why? Is this an appropriate designation for Jesus' followers? Why or why not?

4. The author claims that congregations can be "signs of the reign of God." Do you agree? Why or why not?

5. Is the spirituality of Jesus and his followers "rooted in community," as the author states? What does this mean to you?

6. According to the author, denominations are "a monument to the failure of Jesus' followers to exercise that *shalom* for which Jesus and his friends prayed." Do you agree? Are there positive aspects to our denominational affiliations? If so, what are they?

7. Why does the author relate baptism to "membership in God's reign"?

8. How does sharing Jesus' meal of bread and wine make God's reign more real to you?

CHAPTER 4: *A Spirituality of Caring*

1. Why is the church identified as "a priestly people"? What does this phrase mean to you?

2. What special aspects of your context do you know best? How do they affect the way in which you serve God's reign?

3. What gifts have you been given for the service of the reign of God? How do you use them? How might you use them more fully?

4. What is meant by "a mature faith?" How would such a faith be expressed in the spirituality of Jesus? in your spiritual life?

5. The author writes, "We must give up thinking about worship as a private affair between God and self." Do you agree? Would this change the way you participate in worship?

6. In the author's view, many aspects of church life—worship, preaching, pastoral care—can reflect our commitment to God's reign. Does your experience of church correspond to his idea?

7. What is most significant for you about the case study of FAME (First African Methodist Episcopal Church) in Los Angeles? How is your experience of congregational life similar? How is it different?

CHAPTER 5: *Toward the Future*

1. What is your response to the author's discussion of "reality TV"?

2. The author notes several aspects of modern culture that point to a need for a contemporary spirituality. Do you agree with his analysis? Why or why not? What other events or observations might support it?

3. Do you agree that a meaningful spirituality requires openness to diversity? Why or why not? How does this challenge us?

4. What is most significant for you about the case study of All Saints' Episcopal Church in Highland Park, California?

5. The author suggests that September 11, 2001, may become "the defining moment" for the post-"Baby Boomer" generation. What does this mean to you? Does it affect our understanding of Christian faith? of our spirituality? If so, how?

6. Do you agree that community must be at the heart of twenty-first century spirituality? Why or why not? What are the implications of this statement for you? for the church? How might it change your understanding of God? How might it affect your spirituality?

7. What aspects of Christian spirituality strike you as particularly appealing and/or important for our time?